MARGARET AVISON

SELECTED POEMS

MARGARET AVISON

SELECTED POEMS

Toronto
OXFORD UNIVERSITY PRESS
1991

Oxford University Press, 70 Wynford Drive, Don Mills, Ontario M3C 1J9

Toronto   Oxford   New York
Delhi   Bombay   Calcutta   Madras   Karachi   Petaling Jaya
Singapore   Hong Kong   Tokyo   Nairobi   Dar es Salaam
Cape Town   Melbourne   Auckland

and associated companies in
Berlin   Ibadan

The chronology here is only approximate. Each of the four books which were mined for the selection is the skimming of undated poems written—and revised—through several years. The revision process continued, so that some poems that had been rejected for one volume seem satisfactorily revised by the time the next came out.

My record-keeping has been woefully careless. Thanks to bibliographers and index-makers, the credits have been assembled as best we could—my apologies to any editor who is omitted, and to the publisher for seeming to leave him responsible when the irresponsibility is mine.

—M. A.

CANADIAN CATALOGUING IN PUBLICATION DATA
Avison, Margaret, 1918–
Selected poems

ISBN 0-19-540859-4

I. Title.

PS8501.V5A6 1991   C811'.54   C91-094916-6
PR9199.3.A95A6 1991
75667

Copyright © Margaret Avison 1991
OXFORD is a trademark of Oxford University Press
1 2 3 4–94 93 92 91
Printed in Canada by John Deyell Company

CONTENTS

MARGARET AVISON

SELECTED POEMS

THE BUTTERFLY*

An uproar,
a spruce-green sky, bound in iron,
the murky sea running a sulphur scum:
I saw a butterfly suddenly;
it clung between the ribs of the storm, wavering
and flung against the battering bone-wind.
I remember it, glued to the grit of that rain-strewn beach
that glowered around it, swallowed its startled design
in the larger iridescence of unstrung dark.

That wild, sour air, the miles of crouching forest, those wings,
when all-enveloping air is a
thinglass globe, swirling with storm,
tempt one to the abyss.

The butterfly's meaning, even though smashed.
Imprisoned in endless cycle? No. The meaning!
Can't we stab that one angle
into the curve of space that sweeps beyond
our farthest knowing, out into light's
place of invisibility?

*'This is a revision, because I have learned that 'moth' and 'butterfly' are not interchangeable terms (as I had written them in ignorance in the earlier version), and because the 'angle' seems indicated in Rom. 8:21 and Eph. 1:10'—M.A.

NEVERNESS

OR, THE ONE SHIP BEACHED
ON ONE FAR DISTANT SHORE

Old Adam, with his fist-full of plump earth,
His sunbright gaze on his eternal hill
Is not historical:
His tale is never done
For us who know a world no longer bathed
In the harsh splendour of economy.
We millions hold old Adam in our thoughts
A pivot for the future-past, a core
Of the one dream that never goads to action
But stains our entrails with nostalgia
And wrings the sweat of death in ancient eyes.

The one-celled plant is not historical.
Leeuwenhoek peered through his magic window
And in a puddle glimpsed the tiny grain
Of firmament that was before the Adam.

I'd like to pull that squinting Dutchman's sleeve
And ask what were his thoughts, lying at night,
And smelling the sad spring, and thinking out
Across the fullness of night air, smelling
The dark canal, and dusty oat-bag, cheese,
And wet straw-splintered wood, and rust-seamed leather
And pearly grass and silent deeps of sky
Honey-combed with its million years' of light
And prune-sweet earth
Honey-combed with the silent worms of dark.
Old Leeuwenhoek must have had ribby thoughts
To hoop the hollow pounding of his heart
Those nights of spring in 1600-odd.
It would be done if he could tell it us.

The tissue of our metaphysic cells
No magic window yet has dared reveal.
Our bleared world welters on
Far past the one-cell instant. Points are spread
And privacy is unadmitted prison.
Why, now I know the lust of omnipresence!

You thousands merging lost,
        I call to you
Down the stone corridors that wall me in.

I am inside these days, snug in a job
In one of many varnished offices
Bleak with the wash of daylight
And us, the human pencils wearing blunt.
Soon I'll be out with you,
Another in the lonely unshut world
Where sun blinks hard on yellow brick and glazed,
On ads in sticky posterpaint
        And fuzzy
            At midday intersections.
The milk is washed down corded throats at noon
Along a thousand counters, and the hands
That count the nickel from a greasy palm
Have never felt an udder.
        The windy dark
That thrums high among towers and nightspun branches
Whirs through our temples with a dry confusion.
We sprawl abandoned into disbelief
And feel the pivot-picture of old Adam
On the first hill that ever was, alone,
And see the hard earth seeded with sharp snow
And dream that history is done.

And if that be the dream that whortles out
Into unending night
Then must the pivot Adam be denied
And the whole cycle ravelled and flung loose.
Is this the epoch when the age-old Serpent
Must writhe and loosen, slacking out
To a new pool of time's eternal sun?
Old Adam, will your single outline blur
At this long last when slow mist wells
Fuming from all the valleys of the earth?
Or will our unfixed vision rather blind
Through agony to the last gelid stare
And none be left to witness the blank mist?

PERSPECTIVE

A sport, an adventitious sprout
These eyeballs, that have somehow slipped
The mesh of generations since Mantegna?

Yet I declare, your seeing is diseased
That cripples space. The fear has eaten back
Through sockets to the caverns of the brain
    And made of it a sifty habitation.

We stand beholding the one plain
And in your face I see the chastening
Of its small tapering design
That brings up *punkt*.
    (The Infinite, you say,
    Is an unthinkable—and pointless too—
      Extension of that *punkt*.)

But do you miss the impact of that fierce
Raw boulder five miles off? You are not pierced
By that great spear of grass on the horizon?
    You are not smitten by the shock
      Of that great thundering sky?

Your law of optics is a quarrel
Of chickenfeet on paper. Does a train
Run pigeon-toed?

I took a train from here to Ottawa
On tracks that did not meet. We swelled and roared
Mile upon mightier mile, and when we clanged
Into the vasty station we were indeed
Brave company for giants.

    Keep your eyes though,
You, and not I, will travel safer back
      To Union station.

Your fear has me infected, and my eyes
That were my sport so long, will soon be apt
Like yours to press out dwindling vistas from
The massive flux massive Mantegna knew
And all its sturdy everlasting foregrounds.

BIRTH DAY

Saturday I ran to Mitilene.

Bushes and grass along the glass-still way
Were all dabbled with rain
And the road reeled with shattered skies.

Towards noon an inky, petulant wind
Ravelled the pools, and rinsed the black grass round them.

Gulls were up in the late afternoon
And the air gleamed and billowed
And broadcast flung astringent spray
                         All swordy-silver.
I saw the hills lie brown and vast and passive.

The men of Mitilene waited restive
Until the yellow melt of sun.
I shouted out my news as I sped towards them
That all, rejoicing, could go down to dark.

All nests, with all moist downy young
Blinking and gulping daylight; and all lambs
Four-braced in straw, shivering and mild;
And the first blood-root up from the ravaged beaches
Of the old equinox; and frangible robins' blue
Teethed right around to sun:
These first we loudly hymned;
And then
The hour of genesis
When first the moody firmament
Swam out of Arctic chaos,
Orbed solidly as the huge frame for this
Cramped little swaddled creature's coming forth
To slowly, foolishly, marvellously
Discover a unique estate, held wrapt
Away from all men else, which to embrace
Our world would have to stretch and swell with strangeness.

This made us smile, and laugh at last. There was
Rejoicing all night long in Mitilene.

FROM A PROVINCIAL

Bent postcards come from Interlaken
In August, the tired emperor of the year;
On evening tables
Midges survey their planes of brief discovery
At a half-run. In Milton's candle's light
They so employed themselves.
Some die before the light is out.
Between darkness and darkness
Every small valley shows a familiar compass
Until like all before
Still most unknown, it vanishes.
In Caesar's camp was order,
The locus of their lives for some centurions
Encircled by forests of sombre France.
When day and life draw the horizons
Part of the strangeness is
Knowing the landscape.

INTRA-POLITICAL

AN EXERCISE IN POLITICAL ASTRONOMY

Who are we here?
boxed, bottled, barrelled
in rows?
Comestibles with the trick
of turning grocer, shoplifter
or warehouse trucker, or sometimes,
in faery-false springtime
the lion-hearted four-foot haggler
with a hot dime?

Games are too earnest.
These packaged us-es
are to the gamboling of real nourishment
as mudcake to transmuted sun.
Truth is, men chew and churn (in rows
or squares, or one by one
like a domino on a walled tennis-court)
galactic courses:
chlorophyll, mutton, mineral salts
pinpoint multiple sunrise, and
cram us with incendiary force;
or we ingesting cede
the solar plexus its serenes of sky,
till every sunborn creature
may lume deepforest pools, and floodlight
his architects; find, too,
lenses for micro-astronomical
amaze (he—transport!—
SNEEZES).

Who plunges away
from the inexorable of
weaving orbits, like a colt
hurtled from his gentle pasturing
by a through freight?
(Space with its purple eye
marks his fixed field
and not his helter-skelter heels.)
Fixity of our sun-selves in our courses—
that willed harmonics—is

nothing we know to date,
nothing we know
who do know fearful things.

Look at that platinum moon,
the sky still muslin pale inspiring
doom-sweet violation.
But ask the lone balloonist.
Zones of ultramarine
clutch at his jugular,
and when he engineers his venture,
a Vandal, loving, he lays waste;
the fields and folds Horace could celebrate
strip back to rainsoak
and Rome still baldly suns in its
imperial distances.
(Nothing inert may, in stone, space, exist—except as
our clocking selves insert it.
We move too far from ways of weightlessness.)
Space is a hazard.

Yet this pre-creation density
presses: our darkness dreams of
this heavy mass, this moil, this self-
consuming endless squirm and squander, this
chaos, singling off
in a new Genesis.
(Would it perhaps set swinging
the little horn-gates to new life's
illumined labyrinths if, released
from stifling,
creatures like us were planet-bathed
in new-born Light?)
(Glee dogs our glumness so.)

Dreams, even doubted, drive us.
Our games and grocery-store designs
are nursery-earnest,
evidence.
Strait thinking set us down in rows
and rigged the till.
But being bought and eaten
is, experienced, enough

to change this circular exchange.
And cringing from such courses
compounds confusion:
a new numerical excess
of us-es.

We set up shop after,
poach as we might, nothing else much remained
but tufts of fur and insect skeletons?
And energy hasn't minded
phoenixing for us in our nonce?
But even our own energy
will out. String beans
and coronal pyres of sleep
keg up. These city shelves,
this play emporium,
wobble on nitroglycerine.

If, with dainty stepping, we unbox ourselves
while still Explosion slumbers,
putting aside mudcakes,
the buying, selling, trucking, packaging
of mudcakes,
sun-stormed, daring to gambol,
might there not be an immense answering
of human skies?
a new expectant largeness?
Form has its flow,
a Heraclitus-river with no riverbank
we can play poise on now.

(George Herbert—and he makes it plain—
Guest at this same transfiguring board
           Did sit and eat.)

TENNIS

Service is joy, to see or swing. Allow
All tumult to subside. Then tensest winds
Buffet, brace, viol and sweeping bow.
Courts are for love and volley. No one minds
The cruel ellipse of service and return,
Dancing white galliardes at tape or net
Till point, on the wire's tip, or the long burn-
ing arc to nethercourt marks game and set.
Purpose apart, perched like an umpire, dozes,
Dreams golden balls whirring through indigo.
Clay blurs the whitewash but day still encloses
The albinos, bonded in their flick and flow.
Playing in musicked gravity, the pair
Score liquid Euclids in foolscaps of air.

THE WORLD STILL NEEDS

Frivolity is out of season.
Yet, in this poetry, let it be admitted
The world still needs piano-tuners
And has fewer, and more of these
Gray fellows prone to liquor
On an unlikely Tuesday, gritty with wind,
When somewhere, behind windows,
A housewife stays for him until the
  Hour of the uneasy bridge-club cocktails
  And the office rush at the groceteria
  And the vesper-bell and lit-up buses passing
  And the supper trays along the hospital corridor,
Suffering from
Sore throat and dusty curtains.

Not all alone on the deserted boathouse
Or even on the prairie freight
(The engineer leaned out, watchful and blank
And had no Christmas worries
Mainly because it was the eve of April),
Is like the moment
When the piano in the concert-hall
Finds texture absolute, a single solitude
For those hundreds in rows, half out of overcoats,
Their eyes swimming with sleep.

From this communal cramp of understanding
Springs up suburbia, where every man would build
A clapboard in a well of Russian forest
With yard enough for a high clothesline strung
To a small balcony ...
A woman whose eyes shine like evening's star
Takes in the freshblown linen
While sky a lonely wash of pink is still
Reflected in brown mud
Where lettuces will grow, another spring.

THE APEX ANIMAL

A Horse, thin-coloured as oranges ripened in freight-
     cars
which have shaken casements through the miles of
     night
across three nights of field and waterfront ware-
     houses—
rather, the narrow Head of the Horse
with the teeth shining and white ear-tufts:
It, I fancy, and from experience
commend the fancy to your inner eye,
It is the One, in a patch of altitude
troubled only by clarity of weather,
Who sees, the ultimate Recipient
of what happens, the One Who is aware
when, in the administrative wing
a clerk returns from noon-day, though
the ointment of mortality
for one strange hour, in all his lustreless life,
has touched his face.

(For that Head of a Horse there is no question
whether he spent the noon-hour with a friend,
below street-level, or on the parapet—
a matter which may safely rest
in mortal memory.)

SNOW

Nobody stuffs the world in at your eyes.
The optic heart must venture: a jail-break
And re-creation. Sedges and wild rice
Chase rivery pewter. The astonished cinders quake
With rhizomes. All ways through the electric air
Trundle candy-bright disks; they are desolate
Toys if the soul's gates seal, and cannot bear,
Must shudder under, creation's unseen freight.
But soft, there is snow's legend: colour of mourning
Along the yellow Yangtze where the wheel
Spins an indifferent stasis that's death's warning.
Asters of tumbled quietness reveal
Their petals. Suffering this starry blur
The rest may ring your change, sad listener.

NEW YEAR'S POEM

The Christmas twigs crispen and needles rattle
Along the windowledge.
      A solitary pearl
Shed from the necklace spilled at last week's party
Lies in the suety, snow-luminous plainness
Of morning, on the windowledge beside them.
And all the furniture that circled stately
And hospitable when these rooms were brimmed
With perfumes, furs, and black-and-silver
Crisscross of seasonal conversation, lapses
Into its previous largeness.
      I remember
Anne's rose-sweet gravity, and the stiff grave
Where cold so little can contain;
I mark the queer delightful skull and crossbones
Starlings and sparrows left, taking the crust,
And the long loop of winter wind
Smoothing its arc from dark Arcturus down
To the bricked corner of the drifted courtyard,
And the still windowledge.
      Gentle and just pleasure
It is, being human, to have won from space
This unchill, habitable interior
Which mirrors quietly the light
Of the snow, and the new year.

THE SWIMMER'S MOMENT

For everyone
The swimmer's moment at the whirlpool comes,
But many at that moment will not say
'This is the whirlpool, then.'
By their refusal they are saved
From the black pit, and also from contesting
The deadly rapids, and emerging in
The mysterious, and more ample, further waters.
And so their bland-blank faces turn and turn
Pale and forever on the rim of suction
They will not recognize.
Of those who dare the knowledge
Many are whirled into the ominous centre
That, gaping vertical, seals up
For them an eternal boon of privacy,
So that we turn away from their defeat
With a despair, not for their deaths, but for
Ourselves, who cannot penetrate their secret
Nor even guess at the anonymous breadth
Where one or two have won:
(The silver reaches of the estuary).

TO PROFESSOR X, YEAR Y

The square for civic receptions
Is jammed, static, black with people in topcoats
Although November
Is mean, and day grows late.

The newspapermen, who couldn't
Force their way home, after the council meeting
&c., move between windows and pressroom
In ugly humour. They do not know
What everybody is waiting for
At this hour
To stand massed and unmoving
When there should be—well—nothing to expect
Except the usual hubbub
Of city five o'clock.

Winter pigeons walk the cement ledges
Urbane, discriminating.

Down in the silent crowd few can see anything.
It is disgusting, this uniformity
Of stature.
If only someone climbed in pyramid
As circus families can . . .
Strictly, each knows
Downtown buildings block all view anyway
Except, to tease them,
Four narrow passages, and ah
One clear towards open water
(If 'clear'
Suits with the prune and mottled plumes of
Madam night).

Nobody gapes skyward
Although the notion of
Commerce by air is utterly
Familiar.

Many citizens at this hour
Are of course miles away, under
Rumpus-room lamps, dining-room chandeliers,
Or bound elsewhere.
One girl who waits in a lit drugstore doorway
North 48 blocks for the next bus
Carries a history, an ethics, a Russian grammar,
And a pair of gym shoes.
But the few thousand inexplicably here
Generate funny currents, zigzag
Across the leaden miles, and all suburbia
Suffers, uneasily.

You, historian, looking back at us,
Do you think I'm not trying to be helpful?
If I fabricated cause-and-effect
You'd listen? I've been dead too long for fancies.
Ignore us, hunched in these dark streets
If in a minute now the explosive
Meaning fails to disperse us and provide resonance
Appropriate to your chronicle.

But if you do, I have a hunch
You've missed a portent
('Twenty of six.' 'Snow?—I wouldn't wonder.')

SPAN

The last of the old men of the house of Eli
Had many sons. Both the fat boys
Feasted on festival meats before the altars.
The bullock-sons
And those whose cheekbones yellowed with wine-
    sweat
Knew moister pleasures, under the temple gates.

    First, of the two fat boys,
    Their lips still glistered with repast,
    Eli was reft. He sounded desolate praises
    Far off, among the rocks and stars.

All these, and all their sons—sinews
Toughened, since Egypt, in the rocky pastures
And under the tentskins under the purple sky
East, out of Egypt—
All these would Death smite,
Cheating the house of Eli of chapless age, and the ephod

    The bearded ones feel envy, with remorse,
    And sullied vistas dwindle.

VOLUPTUARIES AND OTHERS

That Eureka of Archimedes out of his bath
Is the kind of story that kills what it conveys;
Yet the banality is right for that story, since it is not a
    communicable one
But just a particular instance of
The kind of lighting up of the terrain
That leaves aside the whole terrain, really,
But signalizes, and compels, an advance in it.
Such an advance through a be-it-what-it-may but take-it-not-
    quite-as-given locale:
Probably that is the core of being alive.
The speculation is not a concession
To limited imaginations. Neither is it
A constrained voiding of the quality of immanent death.
Such near values cannot be measured in values
Just because the measuring
Consists in that other kind of lighting up
That shows the terrain comprehended, as also its containing
    space,
And wipes out adjectives, and all shadows
            (or, perhaps, all but shadows).

The Russians made a movie of a dog's head
Kept alive by blood controlled by physics, chemistry, equip-
    ment, and
Russian women scientists in cotton gowns with writing tablets.
The heart lay on a slab midway in the apparatus
And went phluff, phluff.
Like the first kind of illumination, that successful experiment
Can not be assessed either as conquest or as defeat.
But it is living, creating the chasm of creation,
Contriving to cast only man to brood in it, further.
History makes the spontaneous jubilation at such moments
    less and less likely though,
And that story about Archimedes does get into public school
    textbooks.

THE MIRRORED MAN

Lot put his wife out of his mind
Through respect for the mortal lot:
She having dared to yearn defined
All that to him was naught.

So now we flee the Garden
Of Eden, steadfastly.
And still in our flight are ardent
For lost eternity.

We always turn our heads away
When Canaan is at hand,
Knowing it mortal to enjoy
The Promise, not the Land.

Yet the cimmerian meadows know the sword
Flaming and searching that picks out
The children for this earth, and hurls the curse
After us, through the void.
       So each of us conceals within himself
       A cell where one man stares into the glass
       And sees, now featureless the meadow mists,
       And now himself, a pistol at his temple,
       Gray, separate, wearily waiting.

We, comic creatures of our piebald day,
Either ignore this burden, nonchalantly
(Dragging a dull repudiated house
At heel, through all our trivial ramblings)
Or gravely set ourselves the rigorous task
Of fashioning the key that fits that cell
(As if it hid the timeless Garden).
       I interviewed one gentleman so engaged,
       And he looked up and said:
       'Despair is a denial and a sin
       But to deny despair, intolerable.'

The next week, so I heard, he used his key,
Walked over to the mirror, forced the hand
Of the young man, and left him
Drooping, the idle door of an idle cell
Mirrored at last. Such men are left possessed
Of ready access to no further incident.

      One man unlocked his cell
         To use it as a love-nest.
      By fond report, the mirror there is crammed
         With monkey faces, ruby ear-rings, branches
      Of purple grapes, and ornamental feathers.
         Whatever winter ravages his gardens
      No banging shutters desolate his guests
         Who entertain illusion as he wills it,
      And grant him the inviolate privacy
         His hospitable favour purchases.

      All of us, flung in one
      Murky parabola,
      Seek out some pivot for significance,
      Leery of comets' tails, mask-merry,
      Wondering at the centre
      Who will gain access, search the citadel
      To its last, secret door?
      And what face will the violator find
      When he confronts the glass?

DISPERSED TITLES

Through the bleak hieroglyphs
of chart and table
thumb-tacked for winnowed navigators
who stroke the sable air,
earth's static-electric fur,
who ride it, bucked or level,
master it with minerals gouged and fabricated
out of it, insist
on being part of it, gouged out,
denatured nature, subject
to laws self-corrugated,
created out of it,
through these hieroglyphs and chart
mark with the hearing of the eye
the bellrung hours of Tycho Brahe.

HAS ROOTS

He—Kepler's Orpheus—
a Danish crown, the bishops,
the snarling North Sea night,
bakers of biscuit,
ladies, sweet ladies,
stuffed in their cabinets, swollen with toothache,
the straw and bran
unfabling fields already,
while the Narcissus sun
lends clods a shining:
All somewhere, still,
though they seem lost away
from this weird hollow under the solar architrave.

Are they all only in
those other hieroglyphs
of the created, solitary brain?
borne here in a man-toy?
bounced up, a ball
that chooses when to fall,
comets for hap,
a new respect for the extremes?

Something wrought by itself out of itself
must bear its own
ultimates of heat and cold
nakedly, refusing
the sweet surrender.
Old Mutabilitie has been
encompassed too, wrought into
measures of climbing and ellipse.
This little fierce fabrique
seals the defiant break
with cycles, for old Tycho Brahe's sake.

EXCEPT FROM ALL ITS SELVES

But soft! (o curly Tudor)—
No pith of history will
be cratered in one skull.

The continents, my brother Buckminster
no cramp of will comprises.
The oak that cracked a quilted tumulus
and rustled, all through childhood's
lacey candle-drip of winter,
through feathered morning hours, later
through glass, so that the glassy
exultation of an articulate
stripped rock-and-ribs,
an intellect
created into world, was
wounded with whispers from a single oak-tree.

The periwinkle eyes
of seaborde men
too young for gladness
fade with their shanties.
Lost, like the committing of sins,
crag-shapes are sediment,
chopped down, minced, poured to pave
the shelving
parade ground for pinioned grotesques
in the pink shadow-lengthening
barracks of evening.

THE EARTH HAS OTHER ROOTS AND SELVES

For Tycho Brahe's sake I find myself,
but lose myself again for
so few are salvaged
in the sludge of the
ancestral singular.

Ancestral? Even my brother
walks under waving plumes of strangeness.
The northern centuries
funnel me, a chute of
steel and water tumbling,
and I forget
warm boards, old market awnings,
the two fat little feet in shawls
treading a beaded woman's easy arm
by a sunned stone,
a ginger root
in a stone jar,
a lattice-work of iron
in a dry wind, overlooking
fuchsia flats and the
scorched Moorish mountains,
or holy peaks frilled with cirrus ice
and the slick-paper blues and greens
of their flanks rich
with floral forest.

Forget much more . . .
a name, not the made-name
corrupted to man-magic, to fend off
the ice, the final fire of this
defiance.

> Things I can't know I smell
> as plainly as if invisible campfires
> smoked: a hum of sightless suppers
> on the iridescent shore
> under the dunes. The wanderer's
> sandals ship, and shift, cool sand.

AND 'UP' IS A DIRECTION.

Because one paces (none, now, strut)
one faces sea and space and is
tempted to think: Proscenium!
We have revolted.
Only the stagestruck mutter still
to the night's empty galleries.
Tossed out in the confused up-and-down
too many have casually
fingered the gilt loge fringes,
snuffed into dust the
desiccated peanut-shells
since the last true audition,
and found not even ghosts even in the echoing foyer.

PRELUDE

The passive comes to flower, perhaps
a first annunciation for the spirit
launched on its seasons.

The turning-point is morning:
now Budapest, now feathery
fields—where explorers' maps showed nothing—
now a crippled crofter's in his doorway or
the Scandinavians' by the sea.

Under the dry fence
gooseberries dangled on thin stems,
cottony grass buried the fence-posts, the
grainy dirt trickled with ants.
I smell bare knees again and summer's clouds.

Somebody's grandpa came
in shirt-sleeves, solid
and asymmetrical, rooting the word
'trunk', for a child, as right
for man or tree.
He stood, and gnarled
silently, while he talked over our heads
to some invisible neighbour
we did not bother glancing up to see.

The honeycombing sun
opened and sealed us in
chambers and courts and crooked butteries,
cities of sense.

Tomes sag on the begrimed shelves
locking in light.
Most men would rather take it straight.
Nothing can contrive
accepting. Sparrow in the curbs
and ditch-litter at the
service-station crossroads
alike instruct, distract.

The stone lip of a flower,
the lowest, on the left side,
on the government building,
stares through a different sun.
I lean on the warm stone
and sense its coldness.

The palaces of sense are
patchy after years of hopeless upkeep,
taxes, institutional requisitioning:
a public charge, largely.

A woman with her hair
fixed like a corpse's
is closed like a bank's vault against
even the Sanhedrin of the ranged
windows and towering blocks.

Yet, touched to pallor, she
knows day, abruptly,
as I, and the stone flower, abruptly,
suffer the cryptic change.
The turning-point of morning, and the
unmerging child,
like the sadness of the summer trees,
assert their changelessness
out of this day-change.

Light, the discovering light, is a beginning
where many stillnesses
yearn, those we had long thought long dead
or our mere selves.

In the moment of held breath
the light takes shape:

> now in Osiris, stepping
> along the reedy shore of sunset where
> stone skiffs manoeuvre through
> wild grass and the dark water-gates;

now chipped among the textures of
the chrome, the celanese, the rough-cast plaster,
the stone flower, and my fingers resting on it;

In each at least light finds
one of its forms
and is:

even in the invisible neighbour,
periwigged, black, in hunting pinks,
or rinsing clouts beside the holy river,
who does not bother glancing up to see.

BUTTERFLY BONES; OR SONNET AGAINST SONNETS

The cyanide jar seals life, as sonnets move
towards final stiffness. Cased in a white glare
these specimens stare for peering boys, to prove
strange certainties. Plane dogsled and safari
assure continuing range. The sweep-net skill,
the patience, learning, leave all living stranger.
Insect—or poem—waits for the fix, the frill
precision can effect, brilliant with danger.
What law and wonder the museum spectres
bespeak is cryptic for the shivery wings,
the world cut-diamond-eyed, those eyes' reflectors,
or herbal grass, sunned motes, fierce listening.
Might sheened and rigid trophies strike men blind
like Adam's lexicon locked in the mind?

MEETING TOGETHER OF POLES AND
LATITUDES (IN PROSPECT)

Those who fling off, toss head,
   Taste the bitter morning, and have at it—
   Thresh, knead, dam, weld,
   Wave baton, force
   Marches through squirming bogs,
   Not from contempt, but
   From thrust, unslakeably thirsty,
   Amorous of every tower and twig, and
   Yet like railroad engines with
   Longings for their landscapes (pistons pounding)
   Rock fulminating through
   Wrecked love, unslakeably loving—

   Seldom encounter at the Judgment Seat
Those who are flung off, sit
   Dazed awhile, gather concentration,
   Follow vapour-trails with shrivelling wonder,
   Pilfer, mow, play jongleur
   With mathematic signs, or
   Tracing the forced marches make
   Peculiar cats-cradles of telephone wire,
   Lap absently at sundown, love
   As the stray dog on foreign hills
   A bone-myth, atavistically,
   Needing more faith, and fewer miles, but
   Slumber-troubled by it,
   Wanting for death that
   Myth-clay, though
   Scratch-happy in these (foreign) brambly wilds;

But when they approach each other
  The place is an astonishment:
  Runways shudder with little planes
  Practising folk-dance steps or
  Playing hornet,
  Sky makes its ample ruling
  Clear as a primary child's exercise-book
  In somebody else's language,
  And the rivers under the earth
  Foam without whiteness, domed down,
  As they foam indifferently every
  Day and night (if you'd call that day and night)
  Not knowing how they wait, at the node, the
  Curious encounter.

DEATH

I ask you how can it be thought
That a little clay house
Could stop its door
And stuff its windows forevermore
With the wet and the wind and the wonderful gray
Blowing distracted in
Almost night
And trains leaving town
And nine o'clock bells
And the foghorn blowing far away
And the ghastly spring wind blowing
Through thin branches and
Thin houses and
Thin ribs
In a quick sift of
Precious terrible coldness?

THAW

Sticky inside their winter suits
The Sunday children stare at pools
In pavement and black ice where roots
Of sky in moodier sky dissolve.

    An empty coach train runs along
    The thin and sooty river flats
    And stick and straw and random stones
    Steam faintly when its steam departs.

Lime-water and licorice light
Wander the tumbled streets. A few
Sparrows gather. A dog barks out
Under the dogless pale pale blue.

    Move your tongue along a slat
    Of a raspberry box from last year's crate.
    Smell a saucepantilt of water
    On the coal-ash in your grate.

Think how the Black Death made men dance,
And from the silt of centuries
The proof is now scraped bare that once
Troy fell and Pompeii scorched and froze.

    A boy alone out in the court
    Whacks with his hockey-stick, and whacks
    In the wet, and the pigeons flutter, and rise,
    And settle back.

RICH BOY'S BIRTHDAY THROUGH A WINDOW

Some sod-cart dropped a weed.
Limp, dragging its roots and clotted dust
It lies in the high-altitude main street.

When the squaw and the pony farmer
Walk to the hardware store
Their shadows, smaller and in sharp focus
Seem brisk, alive with tensions
In pulled off-triangle shape.

The cars park in the queen's sun
Like inedible candy.

Upslope, below the treeline
The conifers fade to dry-moss colour,
Old snapshot-blue; below the rockwall
A long score in the mountain's flank
Shows where the open iron seams are worked
Even in tourist season.
The peaks saw-tooth the Alberta noon.

Things of the heart occur here.
Some wilt before sea-level.
Some are tamped down in the
Icelandic poppy beds
Under the cabin-walls.

Tip-alien, rigged like a court monkey
A bell-hop from the railroad chalet
Darts through the sun. And piercing, piercing,
A saxophone shrills on the
Ionic shore, at Marathon.

JAEL'S PART

The mother of Sisera in late afternoon,
Bewildered by the stirless dust,
Cried out, leaning and peering from the window
For Sisera and his spoils.

Its ancient flood weltered with rich embroideries
Dark Kishon billowed to the bloodening sun.

Flotsam of that defeat,
Sisera, out of the Day of Judges, paced
The darkening vineyard, a new alien
In time. The thorny thicket of the vinestems,
Ravaged and leafless, blackened under night.
But the metallic green of the horizon
Stirred in his mind gentle and terrible dreams
Of morning-mists, and a valleyside
Purple with fruit; dreams he had never known
Till now, under the dense dead briary branches.

Sisera's brow, withering with the vision that
Outstripped the Day of Judges, Jael saw.
And to her the olives ripened
And the day hung heavy upon them
And every stone on the ground cast its sharp shadow.
And Jael envied Sisera's cheerless voice
When he came to her, and bade her pour him water.
Milk she brought, and butter
In a lordly dish.

And in her haze-white evening,
Sprawled like a glutton, Sisera
Lay on the tentfloor of Heber the Kenite
Pegged to the dust under the smothering tentskins
By Jael, blessed above women
The wife of Heber the Kenite.

And Sisera's mother stood and stared where the wheels
Of the leaderless warcar scored the leafbrown evening.

OUR WORKING DAY MAY BE MENACED

From this orange-pippery—
Where without violation
We force (the technique is of course secret)
The jumbled fruit to disgorge, severally,
Seed without juice,
Where parakeets are on the p.a. system
And all the walls are wattle
   (Ehyoe hae-dee)—
     Madeleine, off the assembly line—
       which, in the glare and spindle of
       Hawaiian cottons, sea-light, mountain dust,
       and shoals and Takakaws* of oranges,
       is indeed form
       rather than fact—
         Since every cage is freighted
         With apron boys, coffee boys, the ladies
         Who feed and brush the evening shift of parakeets,
   Chooses the extension bridge
   (Windy at sunset)
   Rather than waiting for tiled egress, where the
   Cars debouche, below
   Weavy with green shadow and lamps burning.

. . . Madeleine's mama knew
Her foreman grudgingly, and we
With unrest, sensed, in her,
A certain clarity, a caritas,
But wood-wild. . . .

A person has a nature.
I note hers only that I may bear witness.
Her silhouette high on the span
Focused us then, for the quick—
Occurrence? A hard designation. It was
As if a spoke of the final sky
Snagged her suddenly.
For what seemed only one

* Takakaw is a waterfall in the Canadian Rockies.

Queer moment, she was swept
In some sidereal swerve,
Blotted sheer out of time; then spurned
Back to the pebbles of the path
(After the footbridge), where
Heartstain of sun
Still blurred the airfloor dark.

An evening delegation called, concluded
She is not schooled to cope.
                              It was our guess
She feels perhaps she nourishes a
Shameful little something of a bruise
In at the fusion-point of those peculiar
Burning-wires under the breastbone.
Some of us, privately piqued, privately speculate.

A calling from our calling?
In the economy of the clairvoyant,
Or some high pillared parliament
We gave election, in an elated moment
Too rare for conscious purpose,
Can it have come to light that
The thirst for perfect fruit abroad
Has now been superseded, or subsumed
Under a new, more radical, craving?
Can they have appointed
A locus elsewhere for us?
Our mocha faces are too bland for trouble.

Yet may we, when the morning steam-cocks open
For our new day aloft
Find there is come about a universal
Swallowing-up
(Proceedings against Madeleine alone
Clearly being absurd)?
With only the racks and vats,
The lifts and cages left, uncrated and forgotten,
And the pipes steaming thinly
Under a fading crescent?

THE AGNES CLEVES PAPERS

Why did you come so young
Wearing a cool print-silk, when your arms are round
And your cheek lovely? Why did you meet me here
Where the evening past those muted curtains blows
In liquid verdigris and pearl,
And inside, all the orchestra has played
Is waltz and wedding dance and windy harbours
And the sweets of sophisticated shepherds
Or those in coonskin, leopard skin,
In discus-throwers' oil and olive sun?

What story do you want?
Tales of young love, or of that horse with wings
The pink-striped circus lady rode, standing?
Why should I tell such things
Except to force myself, your peer,
In the strange perfumed anterooms
Of the fastidious voluptuaries.
Have you remarked
How few persist in penetrating farther
And all the rumour that subsides after them
Is of some outdoor chill, some stoney wonder
With monkey-puzzle trees sprouted from paving stones
    And mourning doves over the high wall
        And pomegranate seed spilled in the
           Cleft where sand and winter sun
               Drift to make small regular shadows?

I knew a Finnish student long ago
Who could not come out of a barbershop
And all that glass, without the look
Of a conspirator briefed for furtive action.
His hour was always early morning,
His locus factory gates, and air about him
Was butcher-paper, mottled and saturated,
And an offense to many.
Yet I remember how I envied him
On my first trip, with my thin documents
And no invisible dossier, nothing but a
Statistical identity.

Go home my dear. It is too late
And you are all abrim and pent
And the dark streets are tilted to a vacuum
Where things may happen.

Dour winter scatters salt on the windowledge
And smothers day in twilight, and at Tours
The tower is murmurous with eerie
Barbarian snow; and when the factory sounds
8 o'clock, from my room in the back of the house
I hear black water churning
Out where the street was,
And sense the lumbering passage of
The old black-iron tug in the lost canal
Under a weight of
Smoke, and oil smudge, and snow.
     Stories of Uncle Remus and the carrot-tops
Are used in the unusual after-breakfast
Lamplight to distract the children,
And, when these flag,
Accounts of Uncle, who went to Australasia
And in the far fantailed meridian
Of the Down Under may be this very moment
Riding the surf. Daydreams
Of foam and aquamarine and ochre sun
Disk woodenly about the windowplaces
Where the gray furry flakes feel at the panes
And sidle and sift and mound.
And the pale mother years for
A rocking chair and her childhood by the stove
     The day the postman failed to come
          And chickens froze on the roosts.

Alec drove a twodoor sedan
And worked for the Continental Can;
When you looked at him you knew that he knew
How the blood of a gamebird spilled in snow;
Alone out there on a prairie mound
With a grain-tinged skyline narrowed around.

But Valerius in December could
Simply sit by the fire and brood
And you saw the skywheels turn and follow.

The plum-dark velvets were streaked with tallow
And the morning shine made foreheads grim
And the sword-sounds all were pewter and dim. . . .
Then he would change when the people came
And though sleet fizzed outside, and inside flame
On the logs, he somehow made you see
A thundery midday in July
With all the long lawns violet green
And every wall showing a leaden sheen
And the stillness dancing in violet sparks
Where the tram careened down the empty tracks
Towards the lake-beach and the broad sand
That was bluebrown waiting and warm to the hand . . .
Valerius' mother died last year
And he's gone to Mexico, I hear.

They should have cardgames in the stations:
Those flag-stops, with a crow or two
Slanting about, and a cedar row
Half-dead and silted up with cinders,
And the trainman's car, missing two fenders
And torn in the leather and stuffing half through.
For the soul's voice you need the crow,
But for a man a game of cards
While the planets seed down their big backyards
And the lonely acres ache all round
And apart from the wind there isn't a sound
And the Quebec stove stales the air
Till the eyes stop seeing and simply stare.

Do you remember the vestibule
In rainy September, at five in the afternoon?
Sometimes I feel I have eternally
Been removing my rubbers there, my feather draggled
A little, in the short distance up the walk
From the overheated taxicab. My thoughts
Are fuzzy and whiteish in previous awareness
Of the next hour. I can smell the coffee and hear
China, and ladies' voices, and the sound
Of tires on the wet street.
And I am taking off my rubbers.

In that circular apartment
There are too many doors.
One, for example, gives on a back-kitchen
Although there is no kitchen, and the half-light
Through green glass, and the dust on the preserving jars
And the outdoor chill and smell of paraffin
Are for some reason distressing.
God knows the hall outside is narrow enough
Though the stairs are worse.
Why is it necessary for me to have
So many means of egress?
The woven door in particular bothers me
With all its tall fawn dapper birds, and cobblestones,
And I would be less aware of the black draughts
If it were not there. And the doubledoor in the arc
Behind the daybed should open on
Grass, where the divinity candidates
Could talk, quietly, even by floodlight if need be.
Yet these too give on the hall, where it is scarcely possible
To see one's way, and any hour of the evening
A woman in a bathrobe bearing enamel ewers
Is always just about to disappear.
Tell me, would they object if I stopped up
Some of these doors?

In March you can see the geese from the highroad.
They are very white. The rim of the pond is muddy
And the keen blue of the sky and these voyaging clouds
Show from the round water
And a beat like echoes makes your eyelids flutter.
And red and white collie fusses around the geese
And it would be clumsy walking (after climbing
The new wire fence) to go down there
And why should courage be hailing you to go
Because it is muddy and March and there are a few
Sinewy snowy geese
       Stretching their necks?
The weed that moves here
Its lastyear's withered tassel, under the fencepost,
Will move and move like a silly thing all night.
It is alive. But the wind makes it so.

Stone is a stranger fellow.
Little David had only his stones and a slingshot
Against the giant with the purple beard;
And the onlookers drank stonepure melted snow
And munched their grey beards, there on the chalky ridges.

The old are sometimes savage, brutalized
By scope and newness.
And I am much alone, as well as old,
And fearful sometimes of the tedious fondness
Peculiar to my kind, where the soft light
Plays among things remembered, and today,
Since lighted of itself, must then be subjugated
To venom and timidity.

One evening, just a year or two ago,
The simple penetrating force of love
Redeemed me, for the last perhaps. I've seldom dared,
    since,
To approach that; not that it would go out,
But it might prove as centre of all
Revolutions, and, defined,
Limn with false human clarity
A solar system with its verge
Lost, perhaps, but illumined in
A mathematical certainty
And for my secret I would have a universe.
The need to tell you is exciting
And very bleak.

There ought to be a word cognate with love
For situations people find themselves
As means of coming into their
Foreknown specific gravity.
        No, it's of someone else I'm thinking now.
This plot is not among the magic stories
Although it has their dream finality.

But story-tellers when they singled out
Their characters, found them enhanced
By seablue, or a china nutmeg dayyard.
How is it that by now

The shaft of vision falling on obscurity
Illumines nothing, yet discovers
The ways of the obscure?...

Miss Rothsey, while her parents were alive,
Was an attentive girl, a little acid
Perhaps, and with odd taste in shoes.
Many who might have overlooked her otherwise
Paused afterwards to speculate
Where she came by her clothes—
They seemed an inconceivable cross-breed
By old Assyria out of Peter Pan;

She must have been in her late twenties
When she moved up to Canada.
Perhaps once she had burned her bridges
She wondered why it had seemed sufficient reason
That her brother and his wife offered to share
Their home. For that, they'd seldom seen each other
For twelve or thirteen years. And the strange city
Chilled her. She had once played in
The violin section of the
Cincinnati orchestra,
But now made little effort to discover
Strangers with musical interests
And quickly felt that she had lost her skill

It is banal to draw conclusions
From the garish colours of the poisonous fungi.
Even in terms like 'deadly nightshade'
The pallid horror is misleading.
Poison itself should properly not be thought of
As an inherent quality. There may be
A range of harmonizing chemistry
Where arsenic would be balm and dandelion
And radish sinister and noxious to
Whoever brighteyed may frequent those lit
Elysian hillsides.

Garnet was a commercial artist,
First an artist. Charcoal drawn himself
And by nineteen capable of

Enjoying tea with lemon under
A kitchen wall, in the spent sun,
Simply because he liked it.
His sisters taught him early to
Capture, capitulate to, privacy,
Without themselves knowing or meaning anything.
Under all their family association
Ran an assumed affection
Sweet, murmurous, halfheard under the ice
Of their accepted obligation to
   Be something,
       Be somebody
           (or, in one case, be anybody, in
                  distinction, indistinguishable).
Garnet failed as an artist—
He was the first to cede this little earth—
Because he almost liked commercial art
At times: like geometric pastel disciplines
And casual make-up conferences; preferred
Not to despise.
It was years later that I knew him first
(Perhaps that adolescence is
My gift to him).

Certainly when he hired as shipping clerk
In the export import firm where, for ten years
Miss Rothsey had been in a
Meagre, secure administrative position,
At that time he had promise,
Not as an artist, but as businessman.
His limp striped shirts, and readiness
To ease a crisis, with a printer's apron on,
Hardly endeared him to the freight-shed boys
And did him damage in prestige.
But anybody's hint might have solved that.
He was not disenchanted with the arts
But since his marriage, with two boys at school now,
Wanted more money.
His wife? I met her at the office Christmas—
A sombre, nervous woman, older than Garnet
I'd judge, and absolutely without interest
In us, or registering as Garnet's wife.
A lot of that can simply mean
She didn't want to drink.

Yet it made sense of the long evening hours
Garnet would willingly tackle
If he could have the full lights burning
And joke with the night watchman.
And nobody considered
His working more and more under Miss Rothsey
Was anything his family would have minded.

Do you remember, in the long gallery
At the Museum, the big Egyptian frieze?
What knowledge of the stars or of blood bondage
Or the arithmetic of sacred polity
Delineated morning by the Nile
For the oxdriver or the riverboy?

Garnet made me feel tears, that way.
Certainly he would not have lived
The pious pattern out, husband and father
With neither kin nor keening until death.
Certainly Miss Rothsey never knew
About the tea and lemon, never mentioned
The Cincinnati concert hall,
And neither thought of these things. They cut down
Each other's stature, over affairs of invoices
And policies for the directors' meetings
And at times hated one another.
Yet that is what I meant. Because they met
Each could achieve a doomed specific gravity
And Antony and Cleopatra figured
Ruin in large, but set the style they held.

Down on the levee army boys
Are making breaches in the month of March
To let the January rains pour into
The detour roads and the lamented valleys
And spare all pavingspace
Leaving to rust the lace grill fronts
Of oldfrance New Orleans
And sparing cracked cement
And urban privacy.
The Suwannee River:
Magnolia trees and sawdust yards
And wicker chairs rocking in beaten doorways
With coffee spice and sugar cane

And denims on a line
And the tin washtub left in cinnamon tree-shade
And mongrels thin at ramble and the sound
Of bloodwarm riverflow under the mudbanks:
These are the country seen
Under the culvert, when the sun breaks through
For a short glorious spate.

Rust-coloured chintz, and Taylor-Statton attitudes
Could dominate a foreign policy
Were there no ghostly impetus, no knowledge
How the sea heaved up Iceland out of darkness,
Bleak, and the Altsheim of the elder sun
But thinly peopled.
The long years' march deadens ardour, a little;
Like nine-year-olds we eye clay figurines
That weep at supper on a storm-scoured beach
Under a peacock arc, and could be globed
In glass, and show our faces watergrayed
By diningroom window sunlight, in the safe
Odour of floorwax.

What I saw was an exhibition rocket.
Outside ourselves, time could be purpled so
In one swift trail over the inky grandstand.
The minutes, and the pebbles, and the dream
By daylight snowflakes muffled under pinbone,
Ghastly and very gentle, and the child's knees
Impatient, while he straps on rollerskates,
Are what I found like love, in case
I should see rocket only in my time.

Telling it in plain words
Makes me see how I feared the wrong thing.
The other centre, the known enigma—
All eyes I do not own, contours
That force familiarity where I would
Tumult and spurn like Pan—were the mountain passes
Pure out of thought; this iris bed
Is scarfed in dreadful mist
And no sun comes
Beyond the yellow stoneway....

(Set the pasture bar and close the gate.
The firelight and the cool piano keys
And the silktasselled curtain weight,
And the Shanghai-American marquis
And tires and tiredness, and the dingy freight
Toiling upevening into China tea
Are not distractions. They are the arena.

The scarlet satin tights are your colour
And from the cigargrapebloom of the stands
Radiate black wires down to the floodlit mat
Where the microphone dangles over—any one of them
If you prefer to chew a cigar this round.

How wrong you are to think your glancing back
Into the zones and corridors will long be tolerated
Or, for that matter, looking will lead you back
To the hill and the hoof-pocked dark between
Eveningstar and mushroom.

The wild smell is the other side
Of the impenetrable world of stone
And is no athlete's incense.
After the match is called, before midnight,
We will go dreaming into secondhand junkstores,
Or go for a late sail out beyond the gap
And in the morning, you will see,
The children will be chalking hopscotch on
The Moscow streets, on Lima's cathedral square
Past beaky statue-shadows . . .).

THE ABSORBED

The sun has not absorbed
this icy day, and this day's industry—in
behind glass—hasn't the blue and gold, cold
outside. Though not absorbing, this
sought that:

> sheeted, steely, vaulted,
> all gleam, this morning;
> bright blue with one stained wing in the
>   northeast, at lunch hour;
> in early afternoon
> abruptly a dust-flurry,
>   all but this private coign of place
>   deafened, all winding in one cloth of moth.
> Then space breathed, hollowing twilight
>   on ice and the pale-gray, pale-blue,
>   and far fur-coloured wooden trees
>   and ornamental trees.

Towards sundown
a boy came with an aluminum toboggan.
He worked his way, absorbed,
past footmark pocks, on crust,
up ice-ridge, sometimes bumping
down to the Japanese yews, sometimes
scooter-shoving athwart the hill,
then, with a stake,
kneeling,
he paddles, thrusting, speed-wise, then
stabbing, uphill; then
dangling the rope and poring on
slope-sheen, standing, he stashes
the aluminum, upright, in a frost-lumpy shoal
and beside coasting motorcars and parked cars
listens ... and off again, toque to the eyebrows,
alone still in the engulfing dark.

The inside breathing here
closes down all the window but a visor-slit
on the night glare.

                    New cold is
in dry-thorn nostrils.

Alone, he plays, still there. We
struggle, our animal fires
pitted against those
several grape-white stars,
their silence.

BLACK-WHITE UNDER GREEN: MAY 18, 1965

This day of the leafing-out
speaks with blue power—
among the buttery grassblades
white, tiny-spraying spokes on the end of a weed-stem
and in the formal beds, tulips
and invisible birds inaudibly hallooing,
enormous, their beaks out wide, throats bulging, aflutter,
eyes weeping with speed
where the ultraviolets play and the scythe of the jets
flashes, carrying
the mind-wounded heartpale person, still a boy, a pianist, dying
              not
of the mind's wounds (as they read the X-rays) but
dying, fibres separated, parents ruddy and
American, strong, sheathed in the cold of
years of his differentness, clustered by two at
the nether arc of his flight.

This day of the leafing-out is one to remember
      how the ice cracked among
          stiff twigs. Glittering strongly
              the old trees sagged. Boughs
      abruptly unsocketed. Dry, orange gashes
the dawn's fine snowing discovered and powdered over.

... to remember the leaves ripped loose
the thudding of the dark sky-beams
and the pillared plunging sea
shelterless. Down the centuries
a flinching speck
      in the white fury found of itself—and another—
the rich blood spilling, mother to child, threading
the perilous combers, marbling
the surges, flung
out, and ten-fingered, feeling for
the lollop, the fine-wired
music, dying skyhigh
still between carpets and the
cabin-pressuring windows
on the day of the leafing.

Faces fanned by
rubberized, cool air
are opened; eyes wisely
smile.
The tulips, weeds, new leaves
neither smile nor are scorning to smile nor uncertain,
dwelling in light.
A flick of ice, fire, flood,
far off from
the day of the leafing-out I knew
when knee-wagon small, or from my
father's once at a horse-tail silk-shiny
fence-corner or this
day when the runways wait
white in the sun, and a new leaf is
metal, torn out of that blue
afloat in the dayshine.

A NAMELESS ONE

Hot in June a narrow winged
long-elbowed-thread-legged
living insect lived
and died within
the lodgers' second-floor bathroom here.

At six A.M.
wafting ceilingward,
no breeze but what it living made there;

at noon standing
still as a constellation of spruce needles
before the moment of
making it, whirling;

at four a
wilted flotsam, cornsilk, on the linoleum:

now that it is
over, I
look with new eyes
upon this room
adequate for one to
be, in.

Its insect-day
has threaded a needle
for me for my eyes dimming
over rips and tears and
thin places.

PACE

'Plump raindrops in these
faintly clicking groves,
the pedestrians' place, July's
violet and albumen
close?'

'No. No. It is perhaps the conversational side-effect
among the pigeons; behold
the path-dust is nutmeg powdered and
bird-foot embroidered.'

    The silk-fringed hideaway
    permits the beechnut-cracking
    squirrels to plumply
    pick and click and
    not listen.

Pedestrians linger
striped stippled sunfloating
    at the rim of the
        thin-wearing groves

letting the ear experience this
discrete, delicate
clicking.

THE WORD

'Forsaking all'—You mean
head over heels, for good,
for ever, call of the depths
of the All—the heart of one
who creates all, at every
moment, newly—for
you do so—and
to me, far fallen in the
ashheaps of my
false-making, burnt-out self and in the
hosed-down rubble of what my furors
gutted, or sooted all
around me—you implore
me to so fall
in Love, and fall anew in
ever-new depths of skywashed Love till every
capillary of your universe
throbs with your rivering fire?

'Forsaking all'—Your voice
never falters, and yet,
unsealing day out of a
darkness none ever knew
in full but you,
you spoke that word, closing on it forever:
'Why hast Thou forsaken ...?'

This measure of your being all-out, and
meaning it, made you
put it all on the line
we, humanly, wanted to draw—at
having you teacher only, or
popular spokesman only, or
doctor or simply a source of sanity
for us, distracted, or only
the one who could wholeheartedly
rejoice with us, and know
our tears, our flickering time, and
stand with us.

But to make it head over heels
yielding, all the way,
you had to die for us.
The line we drew, you crossed,
and cross out, wholly forget,
at the faintest stirring of what
you know is love, is One
whose name has been, and is
and will be, the
I AM.

WORDS

Heraldry is breath-clouded brass,
blood-rusted silks, gold-pricked even threadbare
memorials of honour
worn,
a shield when napalm and germ-caps and fission are
eyeless towards colour, bars, quarterings.

A herald blares in a daybreaking
glory, or foolishly carols—
robin under a green sky—or, a
green earth-breaking tip, is still
but with bodily stillness, not the
enemy's voicelessness.

The ancient, the new,
confused in speech,
breathe on, involving
heart-warmed lungs, the reflexes
of uvula, shaping tongue, teeth, lips,
ink, eyes, and de-
ciphering heart.

OLD ... YOUNG ....

The antlers of the ancient
members of the orchard lie
bleaching where the young grass
shines, breathing light;

the candles are carried
to seek out those in the cellars
granular in their lees:

because cobwebs are forked away
and the wind rises
and from the new pastures long after longstemmed sunset,
even this springtime, the last
    light is mahogany-rich,
       a 'furnishing.'

MICRO-METRO

I

Barber's; 'Guitar Lessons'; used
raincoats on outdoor racks,
a many-money-place (closed
for refacing with glass bricks);

ivy-towelled, lonely-sunned,
lawn-folded, hedge-hid
homes; and unaproned
grease-dapper road-grid

all wires, lights, din;
square rooms with square holes
over stores; tea and mutton
smells of our kind: our walls

fall away, recoil
or pile up, a-gape
when the park greens unfurl—
grass rug, *tree* drape,

fountain (drinking), fountain (playing),
foot-paths, benches,
band-stand (but no playing),
a popsicle booth, wrought-iron fences.

II

Under the sun's spots
bandsmen rove
(peach satin, white spats)
littering the grave

slopes with parade-
silks, match-papers, plumes.
The colours are stirred by route-
rallying drums.

They are told what to play
and are dressed, almost ready
to line out the way:
people ... walls ... city.

IN TIME

Stumps in the skull
feel smooth.
No juice. No punkwood.
Sheaves
of tall timber
sprout awkwardly—poplar clumps
        by the railway cut—
in a matter of years.

That's growth.

Smell the leaf-acid
in the new sky.

JULY MAN

Old, rain-wrinkled, time-soiled, city-wise, morning man
whose weeping is for the dust of the elm-flowers
and the hurting motes of time,
rotted with rotting grape,
sweet with the fumes,
puzzled for good by fermented potato-
peel out of the vat of the times,
turned out and left
in this grass-patch, this city-gardener's place
under the buzzing populace's
square shadows, and the green shadows
of elm and ginkgo and lime
(planted for Sunday strollers and summer evening
families, and for those
bird-cranks with bread-crumbs
and crumpled umbrellas who come
while the dew is wet on the park, and beauty
is fan-tailed, gray and dove gray, aslant, folding in
from the white fury of day).

In the sound of the fountain
you rest, at the cinder-rim, on your bench.

The rushing river of cars
makes you a stillness, a pivot, a heart-stopping
blurt, in the sorrow
of the last rubbydub swig, the searing, and
stone-jar solitude lost, and yet,
and still—wonder (for good now) and
trembling:

> The too much none of us knows
> is weight, sudden sunlight, falling
> on your hands and arms, in your lap,
> all, all, in time.

CONTROVERSY

They licked the salt at their lip-edge
and fixed how to feed, sleeping on it
and sweating, and went blind
into the flesh. And some god
you say is God says, 'That lot's lost'
and rolls them loose
like water on silky dust
rolling away (and if some sparrows
      dropt by and pecked at water globules—
      your god keeps accounts, of
      them and their drinks there?)
... centuries gone ... neither here nor there ...
done for ... ('Shove off then').

Judgment? Not His. It's gaming
with loaded dice, & a god made like men
or men with power behind their couldn't-care-less,
and *not* the Truth with the
bite of final cold, & marvelling in it
of bleeding, and waiting, and joy

FIRST

Excessive gladness can drag
the 3-dimensional uncircumferenced circle
out of its sublime true
unless contrition also past all bound
extend it.

In the mathematics of God
there are percentages beyond one hundred.

His new creation is
One, whole, and a
beginning.

BRANCHES

The diseased elms are lashing
the hollowing vaults of air.
In movie-washroom-mirrors
wan selves, echoing, stare.

O Light that blinded Saul,
blacked out Damascus noon,
Toronto's whistling sunset has
a pale, disheartened shine.

If, like a squalling child
we struggled, craving, who
would hear wholeheartedness
and make the world come true?

In ancient date-palm-tasselled
summer, King David knew.
Thus seeds could continue splitting
and oceans rolling blue.

The cinnamon carnation
blows funeral incense here.
In darkness is a narcotic,
a last rite, silenced care.

Can *this* kind of blanking
bring us to our knees?
Christ, the soldiers blindfolded you
and slapped mouth and teeth

asking you 'Who?'
and nothing was said.
You knew.
And knew they needed bread.

The elms, black-worked on green,
rich in the rich old day
signal wordlessness
plumed along the Dark's way.

Stray selves crowding for light
make light of the heart's gall
and, fly-by-night, would light on
the Light that blinded Saul.

But he died once only
and lives bright, holy, now,
hanging the cherried heart of love
on this world's charring bough.

Wondering, one by one:
'Gather. Be glad.'
We scatter to tell what the root
and where life is made.

PERSON

Sheepfold and hill lie
under open sky.

This door that is 'I AM'
seemed to seal my tomb
my ceilinged cell
(not enclosed earth, or hill)

there was no knob, or hinge.
a skied stonehenge
unroofed the prison?
and lo its walls uprising,
very stone drawing breath?

They closed again. Beneath
steel tiers, all walled, I lay
barred, every way.

'I am.' The door
was flesh; was there.

No hinges swing, no latch
lifts. Nothing moves. But such
is love, the captive may
in blindness find the way:

In all his heaviness, he passes *through*.

So drenched with Being and created new
the flock is folded close, and free
to feed—His cropping clay, His earth—
and to the woolly, willing bunt-head, forth
shining, unseen, draws near
the Morning Star.

... PERSON, *OR* A HYMN ON AND TO THE HOLY GHOST

How should I find speech
to you, the self-effacing
whose other self was seen
alone by the only one,

to you whose self-knowing
is perfect, known to him,
seeing him only, loving
with him, yourself unseen?

Let the one you show me
ask you, for me,
you, all but lost in
the one in three,

to lead *my* self, effaced
in the known Light,
to be in him released
from facelessness,

so that where you
(unseen, unguessed, liable
to grievous hurt) would go
I may show him visible.

THE DUMBFOUNDING

When you walked here,
took skin, muscle, hair,
eyes, larynx, we
withheld all honour: 'His house is clay,
how can he tell us of his far country?'

Your not familiar pace
in flesh, across the waves,
woke only our distrust.
Twice-torn we cried 'A ghost'
and only on our planks counted you fast.

Dust wet with your spittle
cleared mortal trouble.
We called you a blasphemer,
a devil-tamer.

The evening you spoke of going away
we could not stay.
All legions massed. You had to wash, and rise,
alone, and face
out of the light, for us.

You died.
We said,
'The worst is true, our bliss
has come to this.'

When you were seen by men
in holy flesh again
we hoped so despairingly for such report
we closed their windpipes for it.

Now you have sought
and seek, in all our ways, all thoughts,
streets, musics—and we make of these a din
trying to lock you out, or in,
to be intent. And dying.

Yet you are
constant and sure,
the all-lovely, all-men's-way
to that far country.

Winning one, you again
all ways would begin
life: to make new
flesh, to empower
the weak in nature
to restore
or stay the sufferer;

lead through the garden to
trash, rubble, hill,
where, the outcast's outcast, you
sound dark's uttermost, strangely light-brimming, until
time be full.

HOT JUNE

People are pink-cheekt only
long enough to
ferret out what if we were wan and wiser we
would let
be.

Give us the word and we worry
it out of its soil and run
off with it
            (IN-FORM) between our teeth
and *have at it* and set up a
branch office to
do it for
people.

And o the zeal of thy cheek,
the tired plumes trailing
home!

Dust composes its late sunlight petals, ribbands, metals,
shorelessness.

UNSPEAKABLE

The beauty of the unused
    (the wheatear among birds, or
            stonechat)
the unused in houses (as a
    portion of low roof swept by the
        buttery leaves of a pear tree
        where a manx cat is
        discovered—just now—blinking his
            sunned Arctic sea-eyes in the
            sun-play)
the beauty of the
    unused in one I know, of
    excellent indolence
        from season into
            skywide wintering
should be
confidently, as it is
copious and new into the morning,
celebrated.

NATURAL/UNNATURAL

Evening tilt makes a
pencil-box of our
street.
The lake, in largeness, grapey blueness
casts back the biscuit-coloured pencil-box, boxes, toys, the
steeple-people, all of it, in one of those
little mirrory shrugs.

The north-east sky too
grows fuselage cool.

On the horizon
ghosts of peeled parsnips point their
noseless faces up,
out; ghost-bodies pile up on each other, all prone, all
pointless, blanking, refusing.

Even the west, beyond the tinged rooftops
smells of cobalt;

      'no—the
      charring of a peeled stick in a bonfire
      is the smell: newness,
      October crackling ...'
large pink children have, all the same, sniffed
the ice in
that quirk of sunset
but refuse
fear.

There is still a lingering
sand-edge of sound
darkness explores.

In hope I say: it is a
listening into a
voice-sound, a voice making with silence.

'Hope is a dark place
that does not refuse
fear?'

       True, the natural night is pressure on my ribs:
       despair—to draw that in, to
       deflate the skin-pouch, crunch out the
       structure in one
       luxuriant deep-breathed zero—
       dreamed already, this is
       corruption.

I fear *that*.

I refuse, fearing; in hope.

TWILIGHT

Three minutes ago it was almost dark.
Now all the darkness is in the
leaves (there are no more
low garage roofs, etc.).

But the sky itself has become mauve.
Yet it is raining.
The trees rustle and tap with rain.
... Yet the sun is gone.
It would even be gone from the mountaintops
if there were mountains.

In cities this mauve sky
may be of man.

The taps listen, in the unlighted bathroom.

Perfume of light.

It is gone. It is all over:
until the hills close to behind
the ultimate straggler, it will
never
be so again.

The insect of thought retracts its claws;
it wilts.

FOR TINKERS WHO TRAVEL ON FOOT

What if it *was* a
verse in the
Epistle to the Hebrews that
kept Bunyan
at concert pitch through
deaf and dumb months?
He found
resonance.
He stuck it out till then, too:
not for one instant sure it
would come to anything, in all his
mute madness, nor ever
diverted for one instant.

'On the one hand'—*N.B.*
        'he was difficult'—
his wife, loyal, was, and no wonder,
hysterical.

On the other hand though—N.B.—
when the sky was
finally sundered with glory
and the cornet
rang out, created stillness,

        he knew it, instantly.
He consented, himself, to
the finality of
an event.

A STORY

Where *were* you then?
    At the beach.
With your crowd again.
Trailing around, open
to whatever's going. Which one's
calling for you tonight?
    Nobody.
I'm sorry I talk so. Young
is young. I ought to remember
and let you go and be glad.
    No. It's all right.
    I'd just sooner stay home.
You're not sick? did you
get too much sun? a crowd,
I never have liked it, safety in numbers
indeed!
    —He was alone.
Who was alone?
    The one
    out on the water, telling
    something. He sat in the boat that
    they shoved out for him, and told
    us things. We all just stood there
    about an hour. Nobody
    shoving. I couldn't see
    very clearly, but I listened
    the same as the rest.
What was it about?
    About a giant, sort of.
    No. No baby-book giant.
    But about a man. I think—
You *are* all right?
    Of course.
Then tell me
so I can follow. You all
standing there, getting up
out of the beach-towels and gathering
out of the cars, and the ones
half-dressed, not even caring—

Yes. Because the ones
who started to crowd around were
so still. You couldn't
help wondering. And it spread.
And then when I would have felt out of it
he got the boat, and I could
see the white, a little, and
hear him, word by word.
What did he tell the lot of you
to make you stand? Politics?
Preaching? You can't believe everything
they tell you, remember—
          No. More, well, a
          fable. Honestly, I—
I won't keep interrupting.
I'd really like you to tell.
Tell me. I won't say anything.
          It is a story. But
          only one man comes.
          Tall, sunburnt, coming
          not hurried, but as though
          there was so much power in reserve
          that walking all day and night
          would be lovelier than sleeping if
          sleeping meant missing it, easy
          and alive, and out there.
Where was it?
          On a kind of clamshell back.
          I mean country, like round about here,
          but his tallness, as he walked there
          made green and rock-gray and brown
          his floorway. And sky a brightness.
What was he doing? Just walking?
          No. Now it sounds strange
          but it wasn't, to hear.
          He was casting seed,
          only everywhere.
          On the roadway, out
          on the baldest stone,
          on the tussocky waste
          and in pockets of loam.

Seed? A farmer?
        A gardener rather
        but there was nothing
        like garden, mother.
        Only the queer
        dark way he went
        and the star-shine of
        the seed he spent.
(Seed you could see that way—)
        In showers. His fingers
        shed, like the gold
        of blowing autumnal
        woods in the wild.
        He carried no wallet
        or pouch or sack,
        but clouds of birds followed
        to buffet and peck
        on the road. And the rock
        sprouted new blades
        and thistle and stalk
        matted in, and the birds
        ran threading the tall grasses
        lush and fine
        in the pockets of deep earth—
You mean, in time
he left, and you saw
this happen?
        The hollow
        air scalded with sun.
        The first blades went sallow
        and dried, and the one
        who had walked, had only
        the choked-weed patches
        and a few thin files
        of windily, sunnily
        searching thirsty ones
        for his garden
        in all that place.
        But they flowered, and shed
        their strange heart's force
        in that wondering wilderness—

Where is he now?
      The gardener?
No. The storyteller
out on the water?
      He is alone.

      Perhaps a few
      who beached the boat and
      stayed, would know.

FOR DR. AND MRS. DRESSER

Your doctor, Lord
from West Irian,
brought pictures of a leaf that served as plate,
and grubs, fat, silkily hirsute, that men
need there for nourishment.
Whoever speak your word
along that coast must share
that feast of fatness first
for love of you and them
who offer from your provenance their best.
The gorge that finds your natural good
in food that squirms is
given aptitude, surely, by grace. . . .

As that doctor, Lord,
learned to subsist, in order
to love first-hand, for you, and tell
how God, to His plain table
invites them too, and will
dwell among them who offer Him their all,
You, once for all,
offered and dwelt—you, fairest beyond call
                of mortal imagining:
here, taking on yourself not only
our spoiled flesh, but the lonely
rot of the rebel, of the solitary,
of all not-God on earth, for all
who claim, in all your range of time. And still

without one queasy tremor, you could wholly
swallow our death, take on our
lumpish wingless being, darkened out
to cold and night—except for
the timeless love
even for us, my Lord.
And having suffered us to glut
the pure well-spring, and having
plumbed even hell, for us, you could
come back, in flesh, living, and
open out the shaft and sweep
of clarity and scope,
flooding us with your risen radiance,
can bid us, now, in turn, o gentle Saviour:
'take, eat—
live.'

JANITOR WORKING ON THRESHOLD

Boot-soles and overalled haunches to the street,
kneeling—
bowed from the ivy-falling, darkly-bright
day-ceiling,
and from cool stone, green court inside—
prising some broken stripping loose, and all in
slow skill, plain sight,
working, till no one need be afraid of falling—

    this street
    and door in the final stilling
    of all (of the one at the threshold with the rest)
    recall the less than the least,
    John, and the wings, and healing.

IN A SEASON OF UNEMPLOYMENT

These green painted park benches are
all new. The Park Commissioner had them
planted.
Sparrows go on
having dust baths at the edge of
the park maple's shadow, just where
the bench is cemented down, planted
and then cemented.

> Not a breath moves
> this newspaper.
> I'd rather read it by the Lapland sun at midnight. Here we're
> bricked in early by a
> stifling dark.

On that bench a man in a
pencil-striped white shirt
keeps his head up and steady.

> The newspaper-astronaut says
> 'I feel excellent under the condition of weightlessness.'
And from his bench a
scatter of black bands in the hollow air
ray out—too quick for the eye—
and cease.

> 'Ground observers watching him on a TV circuit said
> At the time of this report he
> was smiling,' Moscow ra-
> dio reported.
I glance across at him, and mark that
he is feeling
excellent too, I guess, and
weightless and
'smiling.'

CHRISTMAS: ANTICIPATION

For Christmas week the freezing rain
stings and whispers another presence
in the street-lot's unlit needles of wet trees
waiting for Christmas buyers.
The hoar stone
cliff of an unfamiliar church
rises from sidewalk rim off up into
dimming lofts of air;
pigeons flap and chuckle invisibly
up there, when tire-slop and motor-hum
stop, for an odd
moment, and there comes
bird-sound, and the city rain sound falling.

The man newly come home
from university where he was
a freshman, and in love,
slants his face into the smart
of storm, in solitary
pacing, lost from his love, flesh-chilled
by the massive, ornate world that does not matter
because his love is left
out, for tonight and seven more days and nights, and
his heart rocks and swings with the forlorn
lantern of if-daybreak after
heartbreak—the
vision a clam has had—
and it lit him into hope of holiness, a
slit that makes
aching of blindness.

The patient years in the appointed place
brought Zacharias, dumb with unbelieving,
flame-touched, to front
the new sky,
the ancient desert ways
rustling with grasshoppers' thighs, yielding
from dry, spikey places,
wild honey, and a brook starting.

The buyers wedge in doorways waiting for lights, lifts, taxis.
The boy lonely in love moves with the wind
through electric bright, through fading, light.
The old man with his censer, dazed down the
centuries, rays his
dry-socketed eyes, dimming
still, till he could believe, towards,
with, joy.
Down falling whispers
stir in the lopped firs, waiting.

ODE TO BARTOK (by GYULA ILLYÉS)*

'Jangling discords?' Yes! If you call it this, that has
such potency for us.
Yes, the splintering and smashing
glass strewn upon earth—the lash's
crack, the curses, the saw-teeth's screeching
scrape and shriek—let the violins learn this dementia,
and the singers' voices, let them learn from these;
let there be no peace,
no stained glass, perfumed ease
under the gilt and the velvet and the gargoyles
of the concert hall, no sanctuary from turmoil
while our hearts are gutted with grief and know no peace.

'Jangling discords?' Yes! if you call it this, that has
such potency for us.
For listen! there's no denying
the soul of this people, it is undying,
it lives, hear how its voice rises, cries out:
a grinding, grating, iron on stone,
misery's milling, caught up in modulation
if only through the piano's felts and hammers
through vibrating vocal cords—a clangour
of truth, however grim;
let it be grim, if that's how it's given to man
to utter the rigours of truth,
for jangling discord alone—cacophony,
rebellion hounded, hurt,
but howling still, striving to drown
out the unholy's hellish din—
can assert
harmony!

Yes, only the shriek will do—cacophony—
not the dulcet songs however charming they be,
only the discords can dictate to fate:
let there be harmony!
order, but true order, lest the world perish.
O, if the world is not to perish
the people must be free
to speak, majestically!

Thin, wiry, dedicated musician,
stern, true artist, true Hungarian
(held, like so many of your generation
under disapprobation),
was it not deep compulsion, this creating:
that from the depth where the people's soul lay waiting,
a darkened tomb
that you alone can plumb,
that from the pit profound,
from the long echoing chambers down
this mineshaft, from this narrow throat,
you could send forth the piercing note
that rings to the outermost vault
of the ordained, geometric concert-hall,
the rounds and ranging tiers
where remote suns are hung as chandeliers?

Who soothes my ear with saccharine strains
insults my grief. I walk
slowly, in black.
When your own mother is the dead you mourn
the funeral march should not be Offenbach.
A fatherland broken, lost, who dares to play
its dirge, its threnody,
on the calliope?
Is there hope yet for humankind?
If we still ask that question, but our minds
stall, speechless from attrition,
O, speak for us,
stern artist, true musician,
so that through all the struggle, failure, loss,
the point of it, the will to live,
may still survive!

We claim it as our right
as human beings, bound for eternal night,
and adults now—to face up to it straight,
since anyhow the pressure is too ponderous to evade:
if pain is nursed inside,
pressed under, it is only magnified
past bearing. Once we could? We can no longer
cover our eyes, our ears; the winds blow stronger,
to hurricane force.

We cannot hide from it now, nor hinder tomorrow's curse:
'Could you do nothing? why
were you no use?'

But you do not despise us, you revere
our common nature, treat us as your peer
when you lay bare all that to you is plain:
the good, the vile, the saving act, the sin—
as you respect our stature
you grant us stature.
This reaches us at last,
this is our best
solace—how different from the rest!—
human, nothing fake—
this grapples with us, concedes what is at stake
and gives us, not just responsibility,
but strength with it, to withstand destiny's
ultimate stroke, to bear
even despair.

Thank you, thank you for this;
thank you for strength that can resist
even the darkest, worst.
Here at last at rock-bottom, man can stand firm.
Here, the exemplar of the few who seem
burdened for all mankind, gives utterance
to anguish, knows an intolerable duty
to say the intolerable, and thus resolve it
in beauty
This is the true response of the great soul,
art's answer to existence, making us whole
though it cost the torment of hell.

We have lived through such things—
unutterable things—
only Picasso's women with two noses
and blue, six-footed horses
can, soundless, scream
or whinny in their nightmare galloping
what we, just human creatures, here, have known.
No one can understand who has not borne it.
Unutterable things—thought cannot form it,

or speech reach down so far, eternally, utterly down,
nothing but music, music like yours,
Bartok, and yours, Kodály. Music can pierce
this night, your music, music expansive and fierce
with the heat from the heart of the mineshaft. Music endures,
in visions of things to come
when people will sing once more—music, the song
of this people, risen, reborn,
so liberating our souls that the very walls
of the prisons and camps are torn down,
so fervent in iconoclastic prayer
for our salvation, now, and here,
in sacrifice so savage, so insane
to salve us that our wounds are stanched.
To listen and comprehend is to be exalted, entranced
with wonder; our souls are hurled
out of the shadows into a brighter world
of music, of music.

Work, work, good physician, who will not lull us to sleep,
whose healing fingers of song
touching our souls and probing deep
find what is wrong.
How blessed is this cure, how searchingly profound!
We are made whole
when the tempests of pain that batter and throng
in our mute, locked hearts
breaking over you wholly somehow, and sweeping along
the cords of your mightier heart,
issue in song.

Adapted into English by Margaret Avison from the literal translation by Ilona
Duczynska.

*Gyula Illyés' *Ode to Bartok* was written in the autumn of 1955, at a time when
Hungarian literature had come under renewed pressure. After the first 'thaw' under
the regime of Imre Nagy, it was now gradually being forced once more into regimenta-
tion by Ràkosi. Back in power, he personally took the lead in trying to subdue the
writers and enforce 'socialist realism.' At the tenth anniversary of Bartok's death
ample lip-service was paid to the composer throughout the country, while his music
remained largely banned. Illyés came out with the Ode in an inconspicuous popular
magazine containing the weekly entertainment programs of Budapest. The effect on
the public was tremendous. A few days after publication of the issue (some 60,000) the
police on the quiet cleared the stalls of copies still on hand.
    An attempt has been made to echo the sound and syllabics of Illyés' poems in the
English translating.

FARM, AT DARK, ON THE GREAT PLAIN (BY FERENC JUHÁSZ)

Tingling,
sparkling,
smouldering,
over the mute earth the loosed night falls.

Glass-petalled flowers, leaves of thin glass
are incandescent, as
our anguish.

Peculiar weeds, lush and fine-spun
dream on,
half in the dark secreted
their torsos reaching up into the void
like the brooding undergrowth at the bottom of the soul.
Suffering and sin flare up in every blade.
The parts are not the whole.
In the lucid earth-dark all is corruptible.

Agleam is all
that juts up out of the gloaming:
roofslant, poplar,
lip of the trough,
moon-tilted swallow soaring, homing
flittering,
the hay-rick's ripe-gold keening.
Among the stubble pheasants move and rustle,
the young deer nibble.
They shy away from the hare's wide-open eyes
and veer out of the light.

The moonlight's liquid glass
wells over the earth
and quells the very silence in its clasp
to crystal blocks,
glass turrets,
tinkling vine-stems.
Still—how this silence (silvery bushes,
half-guessed-at-stalks, dim files of foliage)
entangles and engulfs the din of empty space
and murmurous flower-scent from the garden-beds.

The house squats
hunched like a scarab, lest
the Milky Way reach down its scaly talons.

The sap in the bean-vines slowly
pulses and throbs
and the withery pods down in the dark recover
a new-born firmness. They discover life only
in building it, never knowing their lot.
Minerals, crystals, water,
the flesh-filling cucumber
drinks in, swelling its small rhinoceros-hide.

While sap (like mother's-blood to a darkling
embryo) seeps through the cells,
whole solar systems circle
within, galaxies countless, crackling
as they plummet and weave:
so, breathless, matter lives.

All things are incandescent with their light of being:
the moon … the moon dwells on its waning;
the breathing tree on how its leaves must fall;
the melon feels its juices sweetening up;
autumn's vinegar-steam the tomatoes ponder;
the corn senses its kernels' thrust from the cob—
they have started already to form
like pearls in an infant's gum—
standing mindless and mild the horses sleep
or dream of trailing down again for water
and the whinnying gallop after.

The sow breathes heavily, deep in her slumber.
Against her belly piglets scramble
and swarm
like a moving pulp of warm
craving, a rosy greediness.
The cabbage-stalks harden and ridge.

Under uprights and open thatch
lie cartwheels, boards, scrap-iron, trash.
The spiderwebs' gauze-cities swing and dangle.
On the warm dungheap the ducks snuggle

and its breath flutters the nettle's candlewick
and nearby wheat and rosemary-spikes flicker.

Stubble, corn, hempfields stretch out all around
far off, where darkness is intense as sound.
The moon shepherds the flocks.
And to the listening field-mouse an assured bull-frog croaks.

I lie in the drenched grass.
Spice-perfumes and my senses here converse.
These flower-cups are metal-froth let cool.
The ground-flow of air stirs
and wafts warmth to me from the stubble-fields,
and honey-smell—
commingled
yet distinct fragrances.
Strange, blissful night, primal, voluptuous—
random—with nothing of passion's single-mindedness.
Plant cannot guess—nor planet—the knowledge a human bears.

Even a man knows little, has but dimly understood
how marble is one substance with milk of dandelion
and prismed insects' eyes
and blood.
Yet, as a man I am removed,
set apart from dews
or Pleiades.
In me alone is the tumult of human cares, and of love—
my pain, my power, are from these.

From the old earth-soaked dark—silence's floor
writhing with stems and storm of sap—to the clear
lift of the upper silences, one free, unbridled power
of teeming: the exploding star
fusing in a primeval shower
of metal-mist, condensed, compounded. Ore
vomited to the crucible where
blast-furnace slag floods off, the slower
seminal globules, crystallizing, or
vegetation's jelly and mulch, its queer
seeds, like the winking elements in the core
of the fissured rock, all crushed in pluvial fire,
molten to become matter, all afire
to become real, till the quarries

of chlorophylled purpose mire
and melt in a plastic flow
and the foam of glossy light
crams to anthracite.
With ululating, jungle-roar,
tremors of flaring fear,
in mawling, ravening desire,
rivered with sweat ... the everlasting flood
seethes and simmers on, in solitude.

I love you. You can be aware of it—
after all, something new,
different from the love helpless matter feels,
with its heedlessness of tomorrow.
No falling star can hear when my heart calls.
The man is sleeping in his corner, the hiss
of his breath catching at a rheumatic crick.
In the kitchen the flickering oil-lamp plays
over the woman as she leans
dozing against the wall.
Her old knuckles and veins
under the lamplight show a yellow glaze.
They are both making ready to die alone,
for this too must be done.

The splayed furniture strains for a voice remote past time.
Sap rises in its dreams.
Leaves sigh, ring wells on ring within.
Whining in sleep, it is washed once more by a forest moon.

A *kapca** by the bed,
beside one lumpy boot.
On the wall a picture from an old paper
pinned flat.
A derelict watch-chain on another hook.
A book mourning, unread.

By now I know for sure what I half-glimpsed before:
how senseless your life would be, all by yourself, alone,
and how it would be for me too, a desolate rolling-stone—
sadness and brute desire.
For animals do not need

---

* A *kapca* is a strip of cloth, wound round the foot, instead of a sock.

to be one till they rot.
They feed, suckle their young, kill, make water, mate,
physical to the hilt.
And when star melts into star, and all the heavens move
the foaming metals flash, and spin, and fade,
the molten passions lapse, dissolve,
all by themselves.
Mollusc and vermin couple just to breed.

Only with you I believe, I feel at one,
nor need my heart at last go so mercilessly alone
to its corruption.

Flower and plant filaments slowly to new
forms glimmer.
The earth bears fruit in an unwitting flow.
Thatch, poplar, cornstalks shimmer.
And I look on as it topples almost in my face,
scaly-bellied, soft, and huge-as-earth,
hiding its reptile head among ancient galaxies,
its tail dangling over in some other night of space,
the jewelled, gelatinous Milky Way, its girth
brushing against the lamenting corn-silk
and the world's bulk.

Adapted into English by Margaret Avison from the literal
translation by Ilona Duczynska.

LIGHT (I)

The stuff of flesh and bone
is given, *datum*. Down
the stick-men, plastiscene-
people, clay-lump children, are strewn,
each casting shadow in the eye of day.

Then—listen!—I see
breath of delighting rise from
those stones the sun touches
and hear a snarl of breath
as a mouth sucks air. And with
shivery sighings—see: they stir
and turn and move, and power
to build, to undermine, is theirs,
is ours.

The stuff, the breath, the power to move even thumbs
and with them, things: *data*. What is
the harpsweep on the heart for?
What does the constructed power
of speculation reach for?
Each of us casts a shadow in the bewildering day,
                    an own-shaped shadow only.

The light has looked on Light.

He from elsewhere
speaks; he breathes impasse-
crumpled hope even
in us:
that near.

LIGHT (II)

That picture, taken from the
wing window, shows a shadow.

High up, between
the last clouds and the airless
light/dark, any shadow is
—apart from facing sunlessness—
self, upon
self.

Nights have flowed;
tree shadows gather; the sundial
of a horizoning hill in Lethbridge measures the
long grassy afternoon.

Still, freed from swallowing downtown blocks of shadow,
I note self-shadow on
      stone, cement, brick,
relieved; and look to the sunblue.

So, now.

LIGHT (III)

Flying Air Canada over
the foxed spread snowy land,
we look where light is shed
from lucid sky on
waters that mirror light.

The magical reflectors there belie
factory   and fall-out   and run-off effluvia.

Where is the purity then,
except from so
feebly far aloft?
Is it a longing, but to be brought to earth,
an earth so poisoned and yet precious to us?

The source of light is high
above the plane. The window-passengers
eye those remote bright waters.

Interpreters and spoilers since the four
rivers flowed out of Eden,
men have nonetheless
learned that the Pure can bless
on earth *and* from on high
ineradicably.

MARCH MORNING

The diamond-ice-air is ribbon-laced
with brightness. Peaking wafering snowbanks are
sun-buttery, stroked by the
rosy fingertips of young
tree shadows
as if for music;
and all the eyes of God glow, listening.

My heart branches,
swells into bud and spray:
heart break.

The neighbour's kid
lets fall his mitts
shrugs jacket loose
and wondering   looks   breathing the
crocus-fresh   breadwarm
        Being—
easy as breathing.

THIRST

In the steeped evening
deer stand, not yet
drinking
beyond the rim of here;

and crystal blur
clears to the jet
stream, pure, onflowing:
a not yet known—

beyond the grasses where the deer

stand, deep in evening
still.

A LAMENT

A gizzard and some ruby inner parts
glisten here on the path where wind has parted
the fall field's silken ashblonde.

I fumble in our fault
('earth felt the wound,' said Milton).
Cobwebs of hair glued
to cheekbone, among
gnat eddies and silences,
I clamber on through papery leaves and slick
leathering leaves between
the stifling meadows.

Eyeblink past blue, the far
suns herd their flocks.

Crumbling comes,
voracious, mild as loam—
but not restoring. Death has us glassed in
for all the fine airflow and the
auburn and wickerwork beauty of this valley.

Somewhere a hawk swings, stronger,
or a weasel's eyes brighten.

The viscera still shine
with sun, by weed and silver riverflow.

TECHNOLOGY IS SPREADING

Two men hatless plodding
behind, in the rain,
one to the other confiding,
set this stratagem:

> 'When using a
> computer it is always desirable
> to stick to one language.'

'These words,' said memory,
'have come unsung—
but note (in case of "always"
or too many a sticky tongue).'

And yet, one 'stuck' to
who could 'desire'?
Just today's luck to
so catch unfire.

Two men, one fair-haired
one nearly bald
passed unimpaired had
while the rain squalled.

STRONG YELLOW, FOR READING ALOUD:

*written for and read to English
385's class when asked to comment
on my poem 'The Apex Animal', etc.*

A painted horse,
a horse-sized clay horse, really,
like blue riverclay, painted,
with real mural eyes—or a
Clydesdale with his cuff-tufts
barbered—the mane
marcelled like a conch and cropped and plastered down like a
merry-go-round pony's
without the varnish—
all kinds confounding,
yet a powerful presence
on the rainy Sunday diningroom wall,
framed by a shallow niche ...

Q: 'Miss Avison could you
    relate that to the "head of a horse"?'

No. No. That one
was strong yellow—almost tangerine, with
white hairs, the eyes
whited too as if
pulled back by the hair
so the eyeballs would water with wind in them,
one you'd call Whitey, maybe,
though he was not, I say,
white ...

Q: 'Auburn?'

It was not a horse-shaped horse,
or sized. It loomed. Only the
narrow forehead part, the
eyes starting loose and appled,
and shoulder-streaming part....
Colour? a stain on the
soiled snow-mattress-colour of
the office-day noon-hour mezzanine
        that is the sky downtown.

Q: 'The Head of the Horse
      "sees", you say in that poem.
      Was that your vision of
      God, at that period
      in your development?'

Who I was then we
both approach timorously—
or I do, believe me!
But I think, reading the lines,
the person looking *up* like that
was all squeezed solid, only a crowd-pressed
mass of herself at shoulder-
level, as it were, or at least
nine to noon, and the p.m. still to come
day *in* day *out*   as the saying goes
which pretty well covers everything
or seems to, in *and* out then,
            when it's like that: no heart, no surprises, no
people-scope, no utterances,
no strangeness, no nougat of delight
                    to touch, and worse,
no secret cherished in the
midriff then.
Whom you look up from that to
is Possibility not
God.
    I'd think ...

Q: 'Strong yellow.'

Yes!   Not the clay-blue
with rump and hoof and all and almost
eyelashes, the pupil
fixed on you, on that wall of
fake hunt, fake aristocracy
in this fake Sunday
diningroom I was telling
about....

103

OUGHTINESS OUSTED

God (being good) has let me know
no good apart from Him.
He, knowing me, yet promised too
all good in His good time.

This light, shone in, wakened a hope
that lives in here-&-now—
strongly the wind in push and sweep
made fresh for all-things-new.

But o, how very soon a gloat
gulped joy: the kernel (whole)
I chaffed to merely *act* and *ought*—
'rightness' uncordial.

But Goodness broke in, as the sea
satins in shoreward sun
washing the clutter wide away:
all my inventeds gone.

ALL OUT; *OR*, OBLATION

(as defined in II Samuel 23:13-17 and I Chronicles 11:17-19)

Where sandstorms blow
and sun blackens and withers, licks up
into empty bright glare
any straggler
           who is exposed
              being still alive,
there:
      clean   cold   water
        throat-laving
          living
            water.

      Look!—a little group of men:
      sun flashes
      on the water poured from leather pouch
      into a bowl, shining,
      now uplifted.
God.
God.
      Saltwater has etched
      their cheeks, their mouthcorners.

WHAT ARE THEY DOING?

They are crazy.   They are
      pouring it
        out.
Sand coats the precious drops and darkens with the life-stain.
                                     Earth's
      slow and unspasmodic swallowing is slowly, slowly
                          accomplished.

No. I do not understand,

yet with the centuries still gaze at them
      to learn to expect to
      pour it out

      into desert—to find out what it is.

SCAR-FACE

Scarred—beyond what plastic surgery
could do, or where
no surgeon was when blasted
in the wilds or
              on a sideroad—

he prows his life through
the street's flow and wash
of others' looks.

His face is a good
face, looking-out-from.

BEREAVED

The children's voices
  all red and blue and green in the
  queer April dimness—
  just as in Ur, at dusk, under the walls—

  are a barbarous tongue, lost on
  that unmirroring, immured,
  that thumping thing,
    the heavy adult heart.

The children's voices are
the immemorial chorus.

WAKING AND SLEEPING: CHRISTMAS

A frontier woman felt
awe, the same awe, she said,
at childbirth and a dying bed.
Yes, said the doctor,
tremblings that reach your heart.

Too few
have to know these enough
and specialties and techniques grow
that ward exposure off.

Isaac went confidently up the slopes
in Abraham's shadow, unaware
until the sacrificer's knife flashed up:
then the branched ram was there.

We carol as our earth
swings some to outer nightward
and sunfloods the Antipodes (sing forth
we both, in seasons sundered!)

The newborn in his mortal fairness
moved those shepherds, and the Asian savants,
from other, usual, bent and stress,
to helpless, awestruck jubilance.

But hard on the manger vigil
came Herod's massacre—like
the Pharoah's once—and Rachel's
heart then broke.

Outside, the hills, sea, sky
wait—mild.　And welling
from past the horizoning why
a new light flows, is filling:

coming far down, away
from the enduring Father,
the Child, alone, sets out upon His way
to the cursed tree, His altar.

    People tremble and yearn;
    our dark hearts thud
    in case that light will burn
    and wake the dead.

SKETCH: A WORK GANG ON SHERBOURNE AND QUEEN, ACROSS FROM A FREE HOSTEL FOR MEN

the hostel's winter flies
where morning spills them out
fumble, undisturbed
by street or curb;

paralleled, walled off, by the force
of the through north-south route,
they never meet
the yellow-helmeted men across the street
whose tangling ways, among
dump trucks and crane scoops, put
down, solid and straight,
the new storm sewer conduit.

Both groups go zigzag, veer,
        stand, wait—

but not the same.

SKETCH: FROM TRAIN WINDOW (LEAMINGTON TO WINDSOR) IN MARCH

Miles of beeswax mist,
     a far ravine with fishbone trees,
      one nearer, peacock's quill-fan with
      the violet batik faintly suggested
         by springtime leaflessness;
    rust-spotted   chipped-paint places,
         roadshoulder, gas-pumps,   and a
               flagless metal flagstick;
    somebody's bricks stashed under tarpaulins,
        a wooden bridge in a field and a black
        dog pottily floundering across it:

the pale wintergreen air has
straw stuck to it, and then again becomes
     dimmed in beeswax mist, a
    visual amplitude so still
        that you can hear the hidden culvert gurgle.

STONE'S SECRET

Otter-smooth boulder
lies under rolling
black river-water
stilled among frozen
hills and the still unbreathed
blizzards aloft;
silently, icily, is probed
stone's secret.

Out there—past trace
of eyes, past these
and those memorial skies
dotting back signals from
men's made mathematics (we
delineators of curves and time who are
                              subject to these)—
out there, inaccessible
to grammar's language the
stones curve vastnesses,
cold or candescent
in the perceived
processional of space.
                    The stones out there in the
                    violet-black are part of a
                    slow-motion fountain? or of a
                    fireworks pin-wheel?
                    i.e. breathed in and out
                    as in cosmic lungs? or
                    one-way as an eye looking?

What mathematicians must,
also the pert,
they will
as the dark river runs.

Word has arrived that
peace will brim up, will come
'like a river and the
glory ... like a flowing stream.'
So.
Some of all people will
wondering wait
until this very stone
utters.

RELEASED FLOW

In the sunward sugarbush
runnels shine and down-rush
through burning snow and thicket-slope.
The spiced air is ocean-deep.

Melting ridge and rivermouth
shape the waters in the earth
and the motions of the light
close the flow as watertight.

                    'In and out the windows'
                    squirrels flip and play
                    through sunsplash and high and low
                    in winter's gallery.

The extraordinary beyond the hill
breathes   and is   imperturbable.
Near the gashed bough the hornets fur
in paperpalace-keep and -choir.

Across snowmush and sunstriped maples
honeyed woodsmoke curls and scrolls.
Sunblue and bud and shoot wait to unlatch
all lookings-forth, at the implicit touch.

MARCH

A Caribbean airflow
shampoos the brook.
The deepsea deepwarm look of
sky wakes green below
amid the rinds of snow.

Though all seems melt and rush,
earth-loaf, sky-wine,
swept to bright new horizons
with hill-runnel, and gash,
all soaked in sunwash,

far north, the ice
unclenches, booms
the chunks and floes, and river brims
vanish under cold fleece:
the floods are loose!

Then sullen torn
old skies through tattery trees
clack, freezing
stiffens loam; the worn
earth's spillways then relearn
                    how soaring bliss
                    and sudden-rigoring frost
                    release
                    without all lost.

EMBEZZLER (I): HIS ACT (Luke 16)

The 'unjust steward'
        called to account
invoked the principle of quid-pro-quo:
a little kindness, scattered in a
mesh of diminished debts and muted
        obligations made a
        stunt-man's safety net.
At least the others' debts didn't seem appalling
        when   his   own   were   plain   past   hope   of   more
                                                        stonewalling.

Anyway, who could honourably venture
fairness to Mammon's lord, being his creature?
His shrewdness actually tickled the manager
and—'good PR'—made the firm feel
taking the loss still worked a general benefit.

The storyteller knew
their world: the rich man and the steward,
customers, sheds, primary industries, the
sea and airways, the
delicate networks of blood, breath's come and
go, the dark lord and the quick
wit too. He knew about people's
nimbleness when caught.

He dares to let the
wisdom of the world
commend that steward's feathering of his nest:
so a closed world of rascals
closes in lord and vassals
with what they choose.

EMBEZZLER (II): A CLASSIC CASE?

The truth is, all we 'have'
is not owned.   How we appropriate
this goody and that, and pad
the books, quick to do favours
from somebody else's coffers!

O yes our accounts look good.

We almost thought that we
had made it, had it made.

When we're called to account
there's—fleetingly—relief:
we really cannot ever make it good.
But quick, before we're out
on the street,
fiddle those final ledger entries
so made friends may provide from well-stocked pantries.

EMBEZZLER (III): '... WISER THAN THE CHILDREN OF LIGHT'?

Taught and furnished richly   but in debt
by not living it out
we can be stiff when caught

and duck the blame
and in haste in another's name
on lesser small-claims culprits lower the boom.

Wasting goods in trust
can go so far it cuts
a man completely off his storehouse access.

Yet who could feed
that steward, fired,
except the backdoor beneficiaries of the same affluent lord?

EMBEZZLER (IV): THE WASTREL BEGINS TO HOPE

But who's really in charge?

The friends he eased
met his necessities
despite his years of waste.

> Brimming hours of days
> and fruit of the sun
> are trusts; also the powers
> in one physique burning, and around him
> in others' energies. All fit
> into a brimming life-ful-ness, an
> everywhere poise of parts in their best places.

To never waste minutes, muscle,
money,
would be to not fail.

Yet, failing, this man still
was not quite wasteful
employing all he had
for those who would be able to provide:
the story does not call *him* 'good'!

> There has been One who proved trust-
> worthy. He does not waste
> a word. Stripped bare to give, He then
> entrusts, awarded all as His possession.

AS A COMMENT ON ROMANS 1:10–

'I saw the Lord always before me.
Therefore my heart was glad and
my tongue rejoices.' (PS.16:8)

Paul petitioned to go
to Rome 'by any means'
and was led by the centurion
to the Emperor's death-row.

Yet he urged it. He was
glad these new Romans existed.
His wisdom was enlisted as
their ally, to find them his.

It did not save his neck
or probably theirs:
he knew beforehand that when light appears
it must night split and earth quake.

THE EFFORTLESS POINT

Three long-distance-runners
out for buoyancy
pad by me, leaving the weed tassles a-waggle
and are past the sumach clump and
fleet,   into brightness flowing,
they bear along
                        lungs
                                    all rinsed with morning.

For Richard Rolle, swift in the strength of stillness,
flowed light,   and the   out there   flooded
his pulses
leaping these six centuries—
love breathes him so alive.

Moving into sky
or stilled under it
we are in the becoming
moved: let wisdom learn
unnoticing in this.

CONTEST

Having in Adam chosen to know
we are sorely honoured in
choosing to know, I know.

We do know what we do.
The second Adam chose to know but
to do otherwise, thus condemning
all but the goodness He
thus declares knowable.

Grimly we concede it, who
would rather do and know,
until as we are known we know.

WE THE POOR WHO ARE ALWAYS WITH US

The cumbering hungry
and the uncaring ill
become too many
try as we will.

Try on and on, still?
In fury, fly
out, smash shards? (And quail
at tomorrow's new supply,
and fail anew to find and smash the why?)

It is not hopeless.
One can crawling move
too there, still free to love
past use, where none survive.

And there is reason in
the hope that then can shine
when other hope is none.

A BLURT ON GRAY

I hear far off the unseen:
in 1940, war
from Canada became
all ear-shell and eye-glaze.

Now, in the small-wars-decades
under the newly rainwashed roof
lying by open windows
I hear far off the unseen
wedding party's horns
within a Saturday of garish and drift.

I remember a 1950 wedding
not far from Montreal, in June:
all alone, in
a deep-green hedged field, sunken
in the steeped lingering light;
the rocky outcrop and bunched cedars
breathed gray and stillness.   And
there, well I knew
how this place framed the tank and flare,
the bloody set-up, booming oceans away.

To hear far off the unseen
can make a here of there
without absolving one from having been
summoned to home   or being
enlisted here at home.

UNTIL CHRISTMAS

When the maiden consented
the angel departed.

All glory was muted
once the shepherds heeded.

The all He created
hangs on this infant—

helplessly human,
son, God only,

light's focus and source
now sped towards the Cross;

yes, and now in glory
quickening love and longing,

till the angel of His presence
becomes our Christmas incense.

THE JO POEMS
JOSEPHINE (SIGGINS) GRIMSHAW

Taking sides against destructiveness
brings on the very evil of destructiveness
unless it is clear that
no two persons
will or should
entirely agree,

i.e.

one must so take sides.

I

THANK GOD, SOMEBODY SPOKE PLAINLY, BUT HUMANLY.

The skills of statisticians
mastered, lead through

The knowledge of administrative law
compassed, leads through

The questionnaires, the tallying,
the scrupulous data, all lead through

to the step beyond quantity,
beyond measurables,
beyond concepts,

out where theory is
challenged by the existence
of persons

     for whom (through
statistics, law, data, wearying
detail, unwearying work)
dignity, the
structures of dignity
may yet be
            provided.

     God help us if we can't remember this.

II

One winter-kitchen place we were, glassed in, under, together:
glass-frames were painted green. The chairs were
painted. Some had curtain-
material cushions on.
The snow-light mushed across from the
                outstretched west. Family and guest, we ate
                a family meal. Then time expanded,
                time to be there.
You wore a cast and
hobbled (newly moved in).
You spoke disconsolately of the city left
behind: 'maroon plush
reception halls, glazed office warrens,
savagely cold, ice-antlering, wire tangled.'
The 'work' was done
but it turned out to be
in-process model-of-work, instead of
honest work. (On Salem Avenue where you
grew up, Jo, awareness comes baldly.)

After good hours, the coffee pot
glued up the oilcloth.
Our cups went cold. Ashtrays overflowed.

III

Today, July 18, 1967,
one troubled night beyond
the time-freeze:
>Jo there, locked in, flat down,
>overwhelmed (alone) with
>waves of total pain—the
>dog shut up in the house lopes between
>the suffering and the glass-panelled
>front door, lopes, hopes to be
>helpful, is
>intent; whimpers. . . .

Husband (from work) and son
coming almost as soon as the city ambulance to the
hospital. But someone else
knew? and long, so long
they did not know.

>So many
>into Emergency, the
>waiting
>room.

A handful of nurses and record-keepers and
one or two doctors. People
sharing dimes to make their calls and
telling each his own story and
helping each other find the washrooms and
apprehensive:
('if you have your own doctor' it
'helps'). So few to help too many
hurt, to answer so
many anxious.
The youthful doctor knows two things:
his human sense of what one being feels,
even the other, the not-himself;
his range of competence, the immediate basis
for making rush decisions on
three 'cases' at once (and hundreds 'outside'
'waiting for beds').
One clouds the other; he feels he must deny
his feeling.

For the young doctor this denial seems
essential to keeping a social trust
(as he works on in his own
corner).

For Jimmy and David, at the moment,
terror polarizes (the
utter need to trust
and angry consternation when a doctor,
        seeing, denies).
(The old father on the telephone
weeping—'I only keep praying all the time'—
to One who once shone forth
against gravecloths and clay.)

Yet my heart chokes on earth.
My questions choke me.
Who could discard any who cry
'I can't believe'—an only mortal truth
spoken in death's presence,
airless in its silence.

The body of death is judged now, will not stay:
        newness will come, at one touch,
        aliveness;—but
there's worse than nothing, any other way.

Coming to that hour
meant choosing to endure
these groanings, too, so choosing, rather than
letting a grave-cloth-and-clay body be
no worse than simple death's, eternally—
if that Cup had been tossed into the grass, to lie
abandoned, and rabbi and friends just slipped away.
But choosing so to die
means, here, and there, through love
life for good in its full power
of resolute splendour.

Teeth set, taking that dare,
facing (among the rest) the questions we
stare at till, slowly, the old horizons
        fill with shining, overspill:

faith, hope, love, are one;
faith is not alone.
One is not alone.

Word spreads. Concern
rises. Helplessness
paralyses. Here is the warm-hearted
loving well-loved friend whose
heart has been open, though
seared by disorientations, danger,
dullness, toothache, the shock of
cultures, and of denials, keeping clear
a beauty almost revealed.

At work. A green
branch and a brick
wall. A telephone-call.
Tears welling wholly for one who 'just
　　　heard', quickening to
　　　　　the too much:
'It begins to seem
as if it is unlucky, knowing *me*!'
　　　(Where is the power
　　　to bear, to be
　　　fully released, fully
　　　available?)

Myself, in the odd march
of these developments: very
practical, very
sensible, very
up and down in emotions. And
evasive, looking not quite at
their suffering, all
three of them
and her father's alone at home,
dimly aware of the
strange pressure of a Presence, of a
prince of this brute, bald,
groan-choked, clammy
time, or of all
in time and out.
Fear. Panic fear.

'Help us
in this thine agony
again.'

Lake blue through
blowing lilacs
deepens skybloom

One dead Lombardy
brooms up among
greenness fresh-billowing
        (bottle-green ditch and
                dandelion: foreground)

The day lifts up
(from full-bosomed loveliness)
our railroad sadness,
tearless,

from behind windowglass.

Josephine, sorely beloved of God,
that day instead of trying to
tell, I found you dying.
        Out in an almost capsized ship, the Lord
        'rebuked' the storm.
        The storm that swamped your life
        so suddenly
        somehow, surely, too, he
        rebuked. Calmness
        unshakeable, came perhaps
        when you lay still, only asked
        for Frodo, that gallumphing animal
        who'd led me to your bed
        through the locked door
        and then lay near, beseechingly,
        fixing us with devoted, steady eyes
        until the ambulance came.

        Abraham knew by faith
        that the boy Isaac mattered—
        yes, to all *three* of them—
        and so could totally risk
        submitting. And
        all three, finally, mattered.

IV

My friend is dead.
She did much good
first in her family also in
her friendships and not least in
tough-minded steps towards
protection for the most exposed,
e.g. the night-shift dishwashers &c.
   who come and go within a week
   too ill   too far forgotten
   to care that 'no work' is
   also 'the worst,' or maybe
   simply not able to recall
   which allnight spot it was
   they should be turning up tonight. . . .

She cried both 'Thank God' on
the day of the attack
when help arrived, and,
in the throes, her head
rolling, through set teeth
'O Christ, O Jesus Christ'—
as I had heard her
over our thirty-one years about this earth
together, in
uncontrollable laughter, in
anger, in
outraged impatience with
unjustness, in
all the bright patches of her
staggering sense of the absurd.

My friend is dead.
Her parents, counting on their only child
say 'Joey's—gone!' as though
she'd skipped again, as
in the black 'thirties she was 'gone' to
marry, game in the teeth
of every kind of—
   cash and in-law and
   Chapel-vs-Catholic
       opposition.

Only now we learn
why she and Jimmy so often
walked hand in hand. He
broke his foot, the day before she died,
stumbling at a curb, and
refused crutches—'I couldn't
see far enough to
put them down safely'....

My Lord, in horrible need I
turn to the Book, and see
sin and death, life in thee
only, and cannot see,
O living Word, I cannot see to see.

I love this friend we've lost.
And the two-dimensional good
that was all I knew
                apart so long from you,
I cannot now dishonour, nor belie.

But the truth brooks no denying.
There is a word, are words,
that do not lie.

My friend is dead.

The Book speaks of a Body:
all that we know of wisdom, art,
insight, perception, released only by
some marvellous touch within the cells
of other parts—from the alerting
        head
all-seeing, hearing, knowing,
remembering, receiving.
Surely this is beyond
analogy, beyond any blunt
ending or comprehending.

A singled body died
the death most shameful,
most grisly, longdrawnout,
exposed, with
two 'other' offenders

also under the emptiness of sky.
A glory nonetheless
shepherded the lacerated clay
from beyond stone to
move and speak, on the roads,
on the shore sands, in where
we are.

My friend is dead.

Already goodness enhances memories.
A goodward life flows strongly
for all our implicit otherness.
        Can one cell be inflamed perhaps, pain-radiating
        from pinch or twist, whatever
        the Evil could devise,
        but in the body still
        active, touched to will?
Long suffering is an ongoing   loving
unto health ('how long
                O Lord')?

My friend is dead.

It is hard, knowing
on beyond your heart,
so slowly, and so little,
                only that
reverence for persons is what
love, truly, can be.

        A place of wrangling roots
        moves the young to petal forth
        nitrogen-breathers on shrunk curly shores with a
        pulse other than
        our lung-cleared veins' and arteries'—

        listening, I almost hear

        The air flows,   lighted and strange,   through
        my nostrils, is
        my present
        but now   not   our
        present.

V

On the doorsill of her death, afraid,
that clear bright Saturday, I prayed
and around four there stirred
pain-brilliant joy, holy accord.
Confident in my will, I waited for
a hospital report, sure of a healthward
turn. They said,
   'Condition poor.' I soared
   away from what they said....

But couldn't there have entered
her hectic solitude an
angelic poured-out joy
visible only as new tiredness?

I do not know. The lift
was real, for me.
And yet I'm not the one
to tidy up a sum as though a
life of intricate bright and dark
and the huge mystery
of loving work, evasions, tactics,
home emergencies, and
sudden sickness, and dying shut off
by the sense-dimming ice-floes
where no one could follow
that I can know—
as though this, in my friend,
or in the lives 'lost' from any 'view'
that truly knows,
as though for them some passages were not part
of the all including.

   The river of Life carves out
    its uttermost channels
   (here 'hardening,' there 'yielding').

YES. BUT.

   These human words burst out
   and will.

VI

Daily and lifelong, Josephine,
you gave voice to the mute
hoping the deaf would hear, who all
too easily, in affluent times,
relegated the poor to a category
(the 'residual poverty' of efficient,
ah, and political, theory).

Having

Sir, you have nothing
        the woman said
Nothing to dip into water
        or carry water in

On the empty-handed earth
the snow stars blot and fur and dwell
        roughing eyelashes of winter grass
        and on the open gaze touching, muffling.
On the snow the slow, rich sun, in time
Seeds   roots   coolness
        through a new sundeep season.

The heart listens.

'You have a cup
when I have nothing.
Both must be
for still refreshing overflowing   new-day
        joy to be.'

The tulips were cherry red.
   now splayed out   they are unable to
      breathe out the light that falls on them.

Boys toss sticks
aloft   where spring
lit chestnut candles. Now   their swollen wicks
lack not even polishing.

Reaping is rough
on field-mice in
the bloodied stubble. Grain is enough
to garner since that only nourishes man.

Dying is fall
of leaf, or day.
A body sculptures desuetude,
outguttering. And yet,   it will,
in time, know everlasting awe.

sky and earth seem to strike each other.

VII PRUNING

Deciduous scented
truck basket, fragrant
branch-loppings in
full leaf, branch springing and
toppling upon branch, twigs
shedding green and wood crumbs on the
curb-line from the truck's trailing
as it starts up at a signal.

Were these branches
diseased? No.
The leaves are squeaking with juices.
Was their tree or were
their trees then
hurt? Can its (or their)
sap flow and diffuse to invisible leaves?
Some trees are trimmed
for buildings or wires, and some
for sturdiness?

Pruning. The
new air
washes in, almost
visual, with
the beautiful, bitter green.

VIII

Wheat and blue sky;
a sloping hill
golden and blue
and still:
            your colours, Jo,
            your clarity.

The sunny snow
of January
your birthday time,
bright, with winter birds
trampling the snow, tilting the limb
of puff-laden tree, and scared
by a quick laugh, a slam
of a door—away!
            your window, Jo.

There need not be, there are
no words for
what is clear.

Now our hearts gather
dear recollections
wordlessly
together.

IX

Only all looking to the core
of life's forever Fire
—no more centrifugally—
can any be.

X

Once there was a court
doomed, and a scheming
truth-anointed, cold
assassin, doomed to succeed
the by then suffocated king.*

It is told that a long look passed
between the speaker of truth and
the one who would soon be a murderer.
The anointer spoke words only
of (truthful) hope for
the victim.

But then he broke down.
The murdered, startled at this weeping,
asked 'Why?'—did he want it named
in advance? it was
focused, surely, on him?

The speaker of truth was wracked
by his people's coming suffering
under the heartlessness of the oppressor.
But he spoke, he submitted in truth
to the Purposer of
what was to be,
weeping, bowed at His knee, not suppliant but
in ever-deepening love knowing
he was not in control,
could not be, would not want to
foreknow more than he must.
He clung to love as the end and so
could honour both truth, and trust.

*II Kings 8:8ff.

142

KNOWN

After the crash we scan
passenger lists—eyes dart
along, down, till at last we can
relax: this horror was not to the heart.

An 'act of God', that tidal wave
or flood—or the lightning-bolt
that caused this crash? We have
His word, yet. He has all, controlled.

Oh, but His eyes are on
the passenger list too;
every mourning child tonight's well-known;
their dead He, nearest, knew.
In charge—and letting us be—but not apart:
for Him this horror is real, and to the heart.

Our horizons stop at those we know
so we can bear it;
His, not at what we know,
compassing our sheer-edge-of-nothing panic
and more; He though in peace and power, knows pain
for time and space, Whom these cannot contain.

MEEKNESSES

An examination room, to the examiner,
        whether medical or academic,
        whether with stretcher and gowned patient or
        young scholars   flushed   intent   submissive,
presents pathos.

The one open to alien
evaluation now is past
risking, given over
to an assessor.
        Waiting on his pronouncement
        tomorrows stand uneasily blank.
To the examiner
the pathos is his
imputed power, too.

On Peruvian plateaus or in the
mountain valleys of Irian Jaya
people with symptoms live, or die.
And wisdom there listens, fingertip sure, alert
to the bright waterfalls, and ponders
the antecedent hidden springs.

MEDITATION ON THE OPENING OF
THE FOURTH GOSPEL

Un-tense-able Being: spoken
for our understanding,
speaking forth the 'natural world'—
'that,' we (who are part of it)
say, 'we can know.'

Even in this baffling darkness
Light has kept shining?
(where? where? then are we blind?).
But Truth is radiantly here,
Being, giving us to Become:
        a new unfathomable genesis.

Come? in flesh and blood?
Seen? as another part
of the 'natural world' his word
flung open, for the maybe imperiller,
in what to us was the
Beginning?

The unknown, the unrecognized, the
invisibly glorious
hid in our reality
till the truly real
lays all bare.
The unresisting,
then, most, speaks
love. We fear
that most.

FOR bpn (*CIRCA* 1965)

The sign on the Library shelves tells it:

LANGUAGE HAS BEEN MOVED.

Look.
Sure enough.

Has been moved over?

(Don't jam in here—
whoever you are, here
where Language isn't . . .)

No.
been moved deeply.

The park fountain is lost, lost
in the pitch-and-toss summer shower.

IT ALL RUNS TOGETHER OR MY SISTERS, O, MY BROTHERS

(thoughts on the days following news
of yet another mine disaster
in South Africa)

'The vital signs are good.'
I didn't want to leave.
Before daybreak you died
while I slept on, and live.

> How clear and bright, that day!
> Everything echoed, rang; then
> the viewless orchestra
> stopped at the tapped baton.

Leaving you, then, alone,
you only minded, then,
if touch then had not gone
for good. I tease my brain
for sense to this distress.
Wanting to hold your life
to the last ebb? and yes,
share, where none can who live?

> Rock thin soil grass mat
> cement an old machine
> walls doors cages and gate
> constitute the Between
>
> for pithead families here.
> (Rescue teams go below.)
> Grip, heart, upon like fear
> with theirs, and weep, and know.

The one I left, those these await
And cannot see:
they, now, are open-eyed with night, to us
unknown, radically.

CROWD CORRALLING

Hard rain.
the bean-mash smell.
leaky tin-brim spill.
grass-soak:

birds clotted in big trees.
Cotton people in go-holes:

uncontrollable beautiful
sheepdogging skypower!

DISCOVERY ON READING A POEM

One sail
opens the wideness to me of the waters,
the largeness of the sky.

'DETROIT ... CHICAGO ... 8 A.M. ... PLATFORM 5'

We queue in long young shadows
for the 8:00 o'clock bus
to the far country.
It finally shows
up at 8:30.

One, when he delays
has good cause:
outrageous care, still hopeful promise.

Does he delay?
            the timetable is not posted.
            The depot is where each is engaged till then.

Why have we less, then, trusted
   this perfectly punctual
      perfectly considerate
         perfectly timed coming

than—at 8:27—we still unquestioningly expected
the 8:00 a.m. bus to the far country?

EARLY MORNING (PEOPLELESS) PARK

An ornament-coloured hound
prances among autumn's
quivering tassels—morning and mist
in swaths, bright-dangled, tapestry
his lissom zigzags.

The paw pads on the grass-mat
are felt, the pads, now, cushion-whispering
pressing softly and swiftly where
sungold is storied,
                    roomed down,
this rich only as touched now.

THE BANISHED ENDURE

A contour map misses
these fine-drawn quarters—
Babylon is gristle-dry
in from its waters and
the lulling fullness of the
silenced songs of Zion.

No watery skies
show on the papiermâché maps.

The young have known no holy city.

Post stalks bald post; wired listeners
sing like mosquitoes.
                    A mighty
river of dark swirls over
bird turret, blank bricked window.

The sinister unknown
binds, leg and arm,
in nightmarish paralysis.
Only awakening would bring release,
the knowledge that there is
a knower, though unknown.

FROM CHRISTMAS THROUGH THIS TODAY

THE Light became our darkness
We rejoiced.

We found we were exposed
and were bemused.

Pointed to Light, the contrast we disliked, we
would have suppressed
the light but He rejoiced Himself to quench it
with all the worst.

Then from the tomb the terrible light
outburst
emptying all we'd gained and He
had lost.

The light that seeks us out
is as at first
But darkness now is different, only ours
by choice.

Child of our years, still help us till we know
the Lamb the only Light.

HEAVY-HEARTED HOPE

Hope's not an emotion,
as *agape* is not.
It is a firm condition
established by one absolute hurt
till the encompassing joy—and that
only for walkers-not-by-sight, each one
in a deliberate devotion.

You grow by going towards?
Yes. Also: growing cells
are the most vulnerable
to cancer.

Pain comes to see
unknowing (awe) not keeping
wild growths of what we think we know
in check. Do we replace a living
with our own fictive person?
Are we forestalling even
hope then?
O, can we err so far?

Heaviness. Fear comes too.
Chernobyl's children are
ours, too, though out of reach,
probably walking still by sight,
dying probably.

No magic banishing
of consequences comes
though they strike only some, and we
are free still.
Hope is not wish-fulfilment.

My hope, not theirs, makes me
look to You more than ever
for hope.
May Your own grieving heart
instruct my cry.

'BY THE WATERS OF BABYLON ...'

Voluntarily in exile
here, among the destroyers of Jerusalem
                    where we panic, indoors,
                    or huddle by the wall
                    hiccupping with distress, blind to all hope,
                    or whirl among the whirlers
                    or hack on at a root
                    to keep the blinkers up against
                        peripheral glares and dread,

You come, to be
unblemished, yet drawing all to
Yourself,
draining all but your ways
        into the cup you purpose to drain for good
that the pure blood-sacrifice
might be forever made
turning all else tombward
till the visible Temple shines
promising that terrible Day
and real walls, real courts, real glory
finally, rise.

BIRTHDAYS

Brambled-in peace, sky-smoking,
wild grass, and the thick springy grass:
this is the birthday-festal
star-correlated hour and place.

There on the green the two
shapely ivory-clear sun-dimmed
children shyly come
each from far off, in wonder.

'A birthday present for me?'
Shyly the gold & ivory said:
'you first . . .' (perhaps too shy
to stir a step forward?).

'Here then'—and clay & ivory thrust
his present on the other little prince.

All the threads of the giver's
woven hidden heart
loosed (like the song of the warblers
in that place apart,

the glory of that garden)
and were all at once a bright
network, and all his being
hushed music, poised, alert.

The other prince, unravelled in a swift
plucking of beaks and cruel talons, was
torn into rustling space.

Black sprang from heart of sun.
Full morning bulged. The glare
faded the garden's delicate-spun
filaments. Landscape lay bare.

'A present, for *my* birthday?'
(numbly). He huddled, close
to the summer grass's bouquet
with its little hidden flowers,

and sighed, and stood. And there,
yes, gold & ivory—coming,
clear as before,
shy, his arms half hiding

his present (new and neverending
treasure, always undwindling
never unsurprising).

From branch sundrench horizon
surging and faintly singing
musics awaken.

LETTER TO DAVID SOLWAY *RE* HIS

THE PIANO IN THE HOUSE IN THE WOODS

Piano in the woods,
in the house in pathless woods:
had it always been there?
so the woods grew thin there
with timbers for surround,
roof; floor instead of ground?

Canada all over!
Keyboard first, then cover.
But by the time you've done it
there's nobody to tune it,
no road, no point. One baby grand and

for a finder's plunder
a surely-musician rumour
only, dying away.

Woods breathe all round.
No twang of snapping strings
no wind-honed resonances
sound.

Now your untheoried words
celebrate the unstoried
quietly turning (verdigris)
among the inexplicables.

A THIEF IN THE NIGHT

A thief? There's nothing here!
   dust-balls, mouse-seed,
   mud-crumbs, even
   motes a sunstreak would discover.
   These the break-and-enter
   artist sweeps clean, invading
   space as its window-polishing
   architect—surprising!

Yet thief indeed where are
   harpsichord, china cabinet,
   hifidelity speakers, humidifier,
   orangerie, wine pantry, who knows
   what all. But the
   break-and-enter man
   was after none of that
   so so much more a threat—
   surprising!

(A royal progress would have been a figure
   more fitting,
   if someone other than the
   'thief' were designator.)

HAVING STOPPED SMOKING

A pile of fingers rests
heavy in the lap.
The pulse, the eyes, exist
active, that's all. Is this
the astral body perhaps?

It's being less than whole
—as who is not?—for capacities
that need stillness twitter, and real
and unrealized powers call
'we're atrophying' in their new unease.

Motor mechanics restore
motors, at a price.
For unpredictable life, a worse
fate is the tune-up than return to source—
or seeing oneself in the glass.

'Hands in the lap, are you
right to lie still?
is this your calling true?'
See, I resolve to go
having grasped the nettle.
Let the fingers dangle.

ALMOST ALL BOGGED DOWN

I

Some scamps are visibly so; their smell
repels their fellows though a few may choose
to exercise kindness, cautiously breathe goodwill—
and yet without ever quite breaking pace.

Some rogues are adequately clean
in clothes and under them, but have their tongues
cankered: acids and sores within;
dread others knowing and so compound new venoms.

A handful shuffle haplessly, prefer
to make the victimizers make their part
plain, for the gain of foreheads clear
and eyes that say, It's not my fault I'm hurt.

The rest? rascals as well, immersed in place
or power or public service; oh, acquainted
with others' taint. Their own they can suppress
secure in the nice role of the anointed.

II

But once always one not one of us
choosing to be of us made every way
we take becoming—dread dally refuse
delight as each one may.

III

Vagrant, in ambush, challenger, masked
or barefaced, everyone at risk
gambles his own way. And the one
of us not one of us is gone
a way some few may following find,
just, one by one.

POINT OF ENTRY

All everybody's time, and my leftover,
    is shaped towards this
      decision, choice, of
  what another, at the worst, wondered
about being human 100% (too): could it be a
    trap? one that we
  nowadays call a martyr complex? or
    a throw-in-the-towel choice to be
      condemned with, part of, the
        doom, failure (100%)? But by a squeak,
          very strait
            very narrow,
you saw it could be too the keyhole light
    you read by thirty years, scroll upon scroll, and
    knew for the crucial heartbeat
      moment, now—
you yourself having over the centuries
    thus deliberated, from
    the point of doom and failure, on,

this, because when my moment
seems come, or coming near,
    though yes I (too?) theatricize,
    swamped so with fakery, fiction, fear,
    yet my keyhole's barely
    seen, and then in in-
      comprehension.

Peculiar life is letting be
because your choice, being mine now
by gift, is
risking rest, mine, by being
    in on your choice who choose forever
      for ever.

CONTINUED STORY

What woman would not know?
    He was gone.
What woman would not try
blindly every device—vigil
by the night window, perfumes—
before facing it? No
lover beloved. Nobody.

Cut off by stone?
worse, cut off by
no visible barrier:
then all the more, her hope
lay dying in her.

What woman would not
scald her eye-sockets with those
painful slow tears, largely unshed?
to have lost even
loss in an
empty new day?

        Whoever did this thing
        is enemy: to me, now—
        and to our friends. (She
        claimed him still in her
                first person.)
        Somebody may know something
        someone can do, even now, even if
        the authorities, having
        acted the enemy, are
        least of all to be trusted in this extremity.

(He had purposed no riddle—
'Did I not tell you?')

        ─────────────
        I don't know. But I saw,
        she cried. He told me to tell you. . . .

        What woman, what man
        dared believe her
        here in enemy country?

A PARALLELS POEM: HEARING

In early afternoon
the cotton print curtains (on
   wooden
rings on a wooden rod)
pulled across, stir a little
against the screen.

This child's mattress
is straw, squeaky. The room
smells of sunned creosote and
   cedar with
traces of kerosene and laundry
   soap.

Sleeping at midday like this
makes one feel large-headed,
   rosy, and
heavy of legs and arms.

Light wanders in droplets and
   little ripples
along the beaverboard,
among the crossbeams.

The very air is mute. The only
sounds are invisible. Then
away off somewhere people
hollering, squealing, calling,
shouting with watershock:
a jazzy blur that
deepens this quietness.

Out of the not long past, who
is heard? Now in our schooled
day we learn, we say
we know. How can we know
who have not heard
and cannot now hear the long
   dead . . . ?

Primordial prairie wind
makes of the first homesteader
a tick on that vast
bristling hide beneath the
   immensities
of breathing sky.

Battle smoke, thudding (hide
   shields?)
bedim the meadowlark; listen—
lament, silence as resonant,
far wedding flutes.

What a hold is in beholding.
Hearing informs the seen.
Unheard presentness defines
   'alone'.
Action is among visibles. Yet

Flesh shrinks to contemplate
the (in a moment) clasp
by a damp swimsuit and
    the assault
of full hot sun before the
    burning
sting of waterpranced spray,
drowsily full of disbelief in a
beach out there waiting.

Alice in her eat-me wonderland
bulged in behind a window
    listening,
heard Bill, unladdered, fallen.
She found out how to dwindle.
She was participating.

Hearing is disbelieving
the dancing lake, is
dreaming what's only here, apart.

Hearing is disbelieving?
In traffic men can walk by ear, through
wet.

In drought, each footfall crackles.
Out in the wilds
one skilled, attuned, can let
the flow of sound surround his peace
till—listen!—he
springs into action.

For a contemplative, must a
sacred hollow place, must echoes
deeply root his
spire of vision?

Hearing alive, though the unseen because
heard in this time although not in this only,
is solitary? it's caught up with
choir and composer, becoming
voice.

DESIGN

God's end is God.
His patience puts it off
(that end) so that the end
may find more safe.

He came to minister
to us—thank God, for His
own sake!—and to confer
on us serving, by us
of Him and His, willing to long-suffer.

'In the beginning, God.'
He now the only way,
though the 'all in all', through
dark that cannot brood
on the impending glory.